Very Sincerely

Manly P. Hall

PATHWAYS OF PHILOSOPHY

PATHWAYS
OF
PHILOSOPHY

By MANLY PALMER HALL

SUBSCRIBER'S EDITION

PORTRAIT ILLUSTRATIONS BY
K. ALEXANDER

PHILOSOPHICAL RESEARCH SOCIETY
3341 GRIFFITH PARK BOULEVARD — LOS ANGELES 27, CALIF.

PATHWAYS OF PHILOSOPHY
is dedicated by the author
to Mary S. Young
as an expression of deep appreciation
and esteem.

Contents

1

NEOPLATONIC METAPHYSICS

2

SCHOLASTICISM

3

NEOPLATONISTS OF THE RENAISSANCE

4

THE ADVANCEMENT OF LEARNING

5

THE MYSTICAL TRADITION

6

THE MESSIAH OF PURE REASON

7

THE NEW ENGLAND TRANSCENDENTALISTS

8

THE NEOPLATONIC RESTORATION

PORTRAIT ILLUSTRATIONS

MAKE PHILOSOPHY THY JOURNEY

Francis Quarles (1592—1644)

A PREFACE ABOUT PRINCIPLES

Under the title *Pathways of Philosophy* we are issuing the second volume of our survey of Neoplatonism. The first part of this work *Journey in Truth* appeared two years ago.

In times of unusual stress, those of thoughtful mind are impelled by the requirements of their own natures and by the pressure of outer circumstances to seek broader and deeper philosophical foundations. Without breadth and depth of internal convictions it is impossible to maintain that serenity of consciousness essential to enlightened living.

Neoplatonism is an idealistic and mystical philosophy, founded upon the doctrines of Plato and his legitimate disciples, and dedicated to the practice of the philosophic life. True learning is not merely the enlargement of the intellect; it is a discipline of conduct—a way of life leading to establishment in imperishable principles.

If we dwell forever in a sphere of effects, content to endure without question the vicissitudes of outrageous fortune, we must suffer the consequences inevitable to this state. There can be no improvement in our condition apart from the improvement within ourselves. Nature has bestowed upon us the means by which we can rescue our lives from the delusions of materialism. If we use these means according to the laws governing them, we fulfill the real purpose of our living.

11

There are eternal and unchangeable principles in the world of causes. We must learn to know them, love them, and obey them, for herein lies our hope of security.

The six portraits which illustrate this work are based upon early engravings and paintings with the exception of Emerson, whose life extended into the era of photography. We have not been satisfied merely to delineate features, but have sought to vitalize the faces of these men with the light of their teachings. K. Alexander has been faithful not only to the line, but has also captured something of the spirit.

We are inclined to think of those great and good as remote and superior, detached by lofty thoughts from the habits of ordinary mortals. We shall understand them better when we realize that they were real persons, who have earned the love and gratitude of mankind because they gave of themselves generously and courageously.

Life will be richer and better for all of us if we will make a *journey in truth* along quiet *pathways of philosophy*.

Manly Palmer Hall

Los Angeles, California. November 1, 1947.

1

NEOPLATONIC METAPHYSICS

KNOWLEDGE AND OPINION

WHEN considering the descent of the Neoplatonic tradition the intellect is forced to cope with an important distinction in viewpoint. The intellectual side of philosophy leads to the perfection of reason, while the mystical side leads to the perfection of faith. In the end faith and reason must be reconciled. Reason leads the mind toward a scientific viewpoint; mysticism toward a theological viewpoint. These modes of thinking have been in conflict since man first pondered the mystery of himself.

Curiously, neither Plato nor Aristotle used any term or word for what we call consciousness. To be conscious is to be aware of self, with the ability to contemplate the existence and condition of the sensations, emotions, mental processes, and physical state of the *self* as distinguished from other *selves*.

To the mystic, consciousness is an attribute or manifestation of the spirit or the soul. To the materialist, consciousness is the testimony of the intellect dependent upon physical existence, and is the source of physical as well as psychical phenomena.

To a Neoplatonist, consciousness is the state of *knowing* as differentiated from *opinion*. To dwell in the security of fact is to be conscious, but to abide in the insecurity of opinion and sensation is to be unconscious in the true sense of the word. As Huxley pointed out, there can be no sufficient foundation for the perfection of the sciences until the true nature of consciousness has been discovered.

Plotinus, the Neoplatonic philosopher, wrote a letter to Flaccus, a student of wisdom, about the year A. D. 260. He opened the epistle thus: "I applaud your devotion to philosophy; I rejoice to hear that your soul has set sail, like the returning Ulysses, for its native land—that glorious, that only real country—the world of unseen truth.... This region of truth is not to be investigated as a thing external to us, and so imperfectly known. It is *within* us .... Consciousness, therefore, is the sole basis of certainty."

The same letter includes an important definition: "Knowledge has three degrees—Opinion, Science, Illumination. The means or instrument of the first is sense; of the second, dialectic; of the third, intuition." From this definition the Neoplatonist established an ascending order of perception as follows:

Opinion is the lowest form of mental activity. It is the acceptance of appearance without question; the mental reaction to sensation without judgment. Opinion was defined by Heraclitus as a falling sickness of the reason.

The term dialectic, the instrument of science, was defined by Plato as discussion by dialogue as a method of scientific investigation, and by Aristotle as the method of arguing with probability and defending a tenet without inconsistency. It is, therefore, a means of thinking, based not upon fact, but seeking to establish fact by judgment.

Illumination in the Neoplatonic sense is a spiritual mystery, the blessed state of the repose of consciousness in the substance of fact. This state is superior to reason and may be attained by intuition alone.

As the foundations of the sciences became more and more dialectic, the intuitional method was almost completely discarded in favor of analysis. Intuition then became an instrument of speculative philosophy. But with the rise of Aristotelianism it lost favor even with the abstract intellectuals. Finding no room among the philosophers, intuition sought refuge with theology. It fared better there, but its broader aspect was stifled by dogma. The final champions of intuition were the mystics (spiritual seekers after the secrets of God) who dwelt outside the pale of academic respectability.

Intuition is the immediate apprehension of the nature or substance of a thing attained without recourse to the machinery of judgment or analysis. It is the power of direct knowledge. It was rejected by the sciences because it was uncontrollable and unpredictable. There was no way in which it could be standardized. Because intuition often dealt with intangibles its findings could not always be checked, and it was regarded as a dangerous cause of mental vagary.

Armed with reason and enriched with the Aristotelian method, the intellectual world set out to conquer time and space. But reason per se is limited by the reasonable, and the reasonable in turn is limited by the reason. The result is a vicious circle. It would be wrong to discount the accomplishments attained by the sciences with their dialectic method, but it is equally absurd to regard their findings as entirely satisfactory.

Twenty-five centuries of dialectics have resulted in the setting up of hundreds of systems of highly specialized opinionism. There are answers for every question that can be asked by a thoughtful person. The trouble is that there are many conflicting answers for each question. You may have your choice; you may cling to Aristotle, or perhaps you might prefer Leibnitz. If neither is satisfactory there is always Hegel, Fichte, Schelling, Descartes, or Nietzsche. But these gentlemen also can prove wearisome, and a variety of theologies may have fascination. The theologians are a disputatious lot, and if you grow tired of their wranglings there are unorthodox sects to invite your consideration. All else failing, you can become hopelessly disillusioned, or turn to the Asiatics for solace.

This decision is difficult. Each school is full of promises, but most of the promises are not kept. Once you accept a school and develop an appropriate devotion for its teachings, the rest is easy. You become a devotee, and it is easy to prove anything you are willing to accept. You become learned, if not wise, and may gain considerable reputation for your skill in argument and persuasion. But first you must accept as a fact something that you cannot prove as a fact. In this decision only intuition can guide you.

All great philosophies must deal with the problem of God; even the materialists cannot escape this dilemma. Deity has been the subject of innumerable discussions, both learned and unlearned. For the most part these discussions have been fruitless and have led from argument to open conflict. It would be pleasant to ignore God and limit the discussions to practical problems of morality and ethics, but how can we classify secondary causes without knowledge of First Cause? How can life be purposeful until the purpose of life is understood?

Faith has been defined as an infinite capacity to believe, and as such it is equally applicable in the spheres of science, philosophy, and theology. The lack of faith is also a belief, in which the mind hopefully postulates negation with the same fervor with which it postulates the reality of a saving grace. Atheism is as truly a faith as theism.

It is customary to hold that the nature of First Cause is unknowable, but there has been no lack of theories on the subject. These theories sustain massive superstructures which unfortunately are no stronger than their basic hypotheses. Yet there is no doctrine so feeble that it cannot find champions who will defend by oratory that which they cannot prove by reason.

Neoplatonic Concepts

Neoplatonism refused to accept defeat in its search for truth. There must be some means by which man may discover the realities necessary to his own spiritual survival. Eternal Providence in its wisdom has not left humanity destitute of formal truth. If the mind cannot attain the real, it is useless to force the issue in the sphere of the intellect. There is within man a power, greater than the mind, which sustains both the intellect and the senses. It is this power that must be the link between the human creature and the Infinite which is the common cause of all life.

All knowledge fails if it does not lead to truth; all living fails unless through it man can discover life. The supreme art is the art of self-knowing, which leads to universal knowing. This is no matter for schools or sects. Many may share in the search, but each must discover for himself and within himself. There is no royal road to learning, to paraphrase what Euclid once told the King of Egypt.

Faith is not merely a static belief in the reality of a universal good. It is a dynamic state of consciousness; the proper means of attaining an inward knowledge of God and nature. We are inclined to think of faith as the acceptance by ourselves of the teachings of some other person. This viewpoint has dominated the Christian world, which holds that there is special merit in mere agreement with the jot and tittle of the orthodox canon.

If man can ascend from opinion to science by putting his mental processes in order, can he not ascend from science to illumination through a gradual process of intellectual refinement? Ignorance is the absence of the knowledge of causes; science is the knowledge of secondary causes, and illumination is the knowledge of First Cause. By this process of reasoning it is possible to extend the consciousness beyond the limitation imposed by the dialectic process.

Plotinus said, "Reason sees in itself that which is above itself as its source." By this definition Neoplatonism affirms that it is possible for the intellect to grasp in part the implication of something beyond itself. Probably this is the highest power of the mind. Like Moses of old, the mind can see the Promised Land but cannot enter it. And like Moses it must come to a lonely death among the hills of Moab that guard the threshold of a better world.

Perchance the supreme duty of the reasoning power is to undo its own mischief and reason man out of the limitations of reasonableness itself. The Neoplatonists experienced a mystery of this kind. While in contemplation, something happened that could neither be explained nor properly communicated. There were rare and beautiful moments when the thinker and his thoughts were one. In such an instant the universe unfolded before some inner eye. There was a complete realization of knowing, doubts ended in certainties, and the power of God filled the mind with an ecstatic beauty. Faith led to illumination, and illumination ended in a perfectly justified faith. Then the experience was gone, the heavens closed as strangely as they had opened, the sense of vastness diminished, and the thinker was again locked inside the narrow walls of his own thoughts.

Although the mystical experience lasted only an instant, its effect endured throughout life. Every part of the being testified to the reality of this extension of spiritual power. A certainty was set up in the center of the self, and this strength transformed the human being into what the Greeks called a Hero. All questions were answered; all doubts were solved by this fleeting glimpse of eternal values.

The majority of Neoplatonists were men of outstanding intellect. They examined the circumstances involved in the mystical experience in so far as these circumstances were susceptible of analysis. They learned that the mystical experience was most likely to come to idealists who were consecrated to the love of God, the service of beauty, and the practice of charitable works. The direct cause of illumination, therefore, was a spiritual way of life.

Following this thought to its reasonable conclusion they were able to define philosophy as not only an intellectual exercise but as a way of living. Philosophy was dependent upon the philosopher. If his deportment was inconsistent with the laws of life his intellectual labors were in vain. This was the reason for setting up the philosophical discipline. The intellect must be freed from the burden of nonessentials. All destructive thoughts must be overcome. The universe dwelt in a condition of eternal peace. Man must bring himself to the same condition if he would experience the mystical union. The proud and the worldly-wise had no stillness in themselves. Burdened with their own conceits, it was not possible for them to know the gentleness of the spirit. Hence all allegiance to confusion was detrimental to true insight.

But the Neoplatonists did not share the views of some sects that all learning was dangerous and that Deity was particularly lenient toward the uninformed. Philosophy was a moral discipline for the realization of calmness and peace. Through learning, the mind came to be content with stillness and repose. True learning brought dissension to an end. This was its special purpose. When wisdom ended fear it removed the internal obstacle to tranquillity. When reason terminated selfishness and avarice man's inner calm increased and he was fitted for mystical experience.

To quote again from the letter of Plotinus: "You ask how we can know the Infinite? I answer, not by reason. It is the office of reason to distinguish and define. The Infinite, therefore, cannot be ranked among its objects. You can only apprehend the Infinite by a faculty superior to reason, by entering into a state in which you are your finite self no longer, in which the Divine Essence is communicated to you. This is ecstasy. It is liberation of your mind from its finite consciousness. Like only can apprehend like; when you thus cease to be finite, you become one with the Infinite."

It would be difficult to discover a more complete exposition of the mystical formula. It is surprising, therefore, that philosophical mysticism has not exercised a larger influence in the molding of our cultural life. The only explanation is that which we have already given in Volume I of this work. The mere contemplation of mystical fact is beyond the experience limitation of the average individual. He does not attempt union with First Cause because he does not realize the significance of such a union. Man strives only after that which he regards as necessary. None but the enlightened thinker has found illumination necessary to the perfection of his own life and the security of world-civilization.

The classical thinkers observed that the material sphere exercises an hypnotic influence on the souls enmeshed in its substances. A lassitude attacks the inner perceptions, dulling their power and resulting in patience and resignation to the pressure of circumstances. Human beings become like herds of animals roaming about the earth in search of favorable pastures. For such as these, life is important only in terms of creature comforts. But they seek in vain, for there will be no solution to the physical problems of the human race until the lethargy of the soul is overcome by philosophical discipline.

It is obvious that such speculations are reserved for the philosophic elect, and are meaningless to the masses. For this reason the initiates of the Mysteries were called shepherds. They were the keepers of the flocks that grazed on the green slopes of Olympus, unaware of the temple on the farther peak. The psychopomps (soul conductors) guarded the herds of souls that flowed into the material world from the ethers of space. Only these leaders knew the way of the

If man were by nature a creature of the earth, the earth could satisfy him. But he is a creature of heaven, his soul originating among the stars. Even in his ignorance he aspires to a state of being which the earth cannot bestow. All of his questions are asked here, but the answers lie elsewhere. Personal problems bear witness to universal principles, and personal happiness requires universal adjustments for its attainment.

gods, which they had discovered through purification and contemplation.

The Neoplatonists described their mystical exaltation as a participation in the Universal Identity. Of this ineffable state Plotinus wrote: "But this sublime condition is not of permanent duration. It is only now and then that we can enjoy this elevation (mercifully made possible for us) above the limits of the body and the world. I myself have realized it but three times as yet, and Porphyry hitherto not once. All that tends to purify and elevate the mind will assist you in this attainment, and facilitate the approach and the recurrence of these happy intervals. There are, then, different roads by which this end may be reached. The love of beauty which exalts the poet; that devotion to the One and that ascent of science which makes the ambition of the philosopher; and that love and those prayers by which some devout and ardent soul tends in its moral purity towards perfection. These are the great highways conducting to that height above the actual and the particular where we stand in the immediate presence of the Infinite, who shines out as from the depth of the soul."

The Mystical Experience

Here Plotinus emphasizes two important points. First, the mystical experience cannot be summoned or demanded by the intellect, but must be bestowed by the gods. This thought could easily be misunderstood by the uninformed as being contrary to the law of cause and effect, which operates according to merit alone. But there is no real contradiction. The term God, or Providence, or Divine Will, means the perfect working of universal law. It is not that the law is eccentric, but that man is incapable of accurately estimating the degree of his own adjustment with the pattern of the world soul.

It is quite natural that the sincere student who practices the virtues of philosophy to the best of his understanding should expect to be rewarded by extension of consciousness. If this extension does not come when and as he believes it should come, he is inclined to feel that the gods are withholding that which is rightfully his. But how can man know his own spiritual progress, and what right has he to pass judgment upon the unknown? Illumination comes not when it is expected, but when the human soul is ready to receive it. No man knows the hour when the Lord of Light will come, nor should this be of particular concern. The duty of the disciple is to prepare himself, and abide in the simple faith that the universe will fulfill its work.

The second point which Plotinus indicates is the diversity of means by which the unity of ends may be accomplished. Mysticism is not dependent upon any particular discipline, because the end to be attained is not a particular. All self-discipline leads toward the reasonable end of discipline—enlightenment. Perhaps it will be well to consider the term discipline as it is used in the Neoplatonic system.

We are inclined to think of discipline as the exercise of the will over behavior. The term is loaded with the implication of self-control and the inhibition of violent extremes of temperament. But this is not the philosophical meaning of the word. Rather it means the successive stages of enlightenment releasing successive degrees of human integrity. Discipline is release—not control.

For an example, let us take the problem of virtue. What does the word mean? Each individual will have a different definition according to his own experience and the environment in which he lives. If a man should say to us "Be virtuous" he confronts our minds with an abstraction beyond human comprehension. If we attempt to obey this indefinite order it is likely that we shall endeavor to correct a variety of general faults by imposing upon them the inhibiting power of will-conviction. In the end we become neurotic rather than virtuous.

Neoplatonic discipline is an adventure toward the discovery of the *one*, the *beautiful*, and the *good* in all things. The illusion of diversity is overcome by the realization of unity or oneness. The illusion of disorder is overcome by the realization of beauty. The illusion of evil is overcome by the realization of good. We grow by expanding our perceptive and reflective faculties toward the divine in all nature and things. This is the true mystical discipline. We possess the power to discover that which we sincerely desire. The right desire is therefore most important.

It is not difficult to understand why the mystical experience is not common among the scientists and scholars of today. They have no spiritual desire, only an academic inquisitiveness. Certainly they want to know the answers to their questions, but they have no deep and abiding love for either the subject or the object of their search. They would find unity by increasing the illusion of diversity. They would discover the *one* by continually breaking it up into smaller and more numerous parts.

There can be no mysticism without love. In *The Banquet* Plato defines love as the child of poverty and plenty. When man turns his affections toward God he becomes aware of a twofold mystery; first, the poverty in himself, and second, the plentitude in God. This realization is one of the first of the mystical experiences that can come to man.

Love, Neoplatonically defined, is the natural emotion of man to man, and of all men to God. Human love is based on the dependence of one person upon another, and divine love is the dependence of all creatures upon their Heavenly Father. There can be no true religion without love, which St. Paul tells us "suffereth long and is kind."

The power of love originates in the sympathy which exists between similars throughout nature. The soul is the throne of love. A part of the world soul abides in every creature. The natural motion of the parts is due to their desire for wholeness; they long to be restored to the world soul from which they came. This longing is aspiration, which is the impulse behind all growth. The realization of the love of God in the abstract is impossible without the realization of the love of our fellow creatures in the particulars of daily living. Through the lesser experience we partake of the greater mystery.

Dionysius Areopagiticus

The effect of Neoplatonism upon the early Christian Church was deep and lasting. Consider the case of Dionysius Areopagiticus, one of the Athenians who listened to the preaching of St. Paul at the Hill of Mars. Very little is known about Dionysius except that Eusebius credits him with being the first bishop of Athens. About the middle of the 4th century four books and a number of letters were circulated under the name of Dionysius the Areopagite. The most famous of these writings is titled *On Mystic Theology*. The true author of these works is unknown, but it is usual to refer to him as the pseudo-Dionysius. This phantom philosopher was evidently a man of outstanding intellectual attainments. He has blended together into a beautiful and inspiring system the Christian, Jewish, Oriental, and Classical Greek learning. The framework is typically Neoplatonic, and while Christian terms replace the old pagan categories, the principles involved remain practically unchanged.

In the Dionysian writings three hierarchies of celestial beings surround the throne of the triune God. The first hierarchy consists of the Seraphim, the Cherubim, and the Thrones. These exalted creatures stand in the presence of the Divine Glory and reflect its light upon the second hierarchy. This consists of the Dominations, Virtues, and Powers. These great orders of life reflect their powers downward to the third hierarchy, which is composed of the Principalities, Archangels, and Angels. The third group is concerned principally with the needs of humanity, and is the particular ruler of the mundane sphere.

The celestial hierarchy is reflected upon the earth as the ecclesiastical hierarchy, which is founded in Jesus and descends through the sacraments to the officers of the Church. In this arrangement the third hierarchy is made up of the monks, whose duty it is to minister to the needs of the uninitiated laity.

About the year A. D. 847 the books of the pseudo-Dionysius came into prominence in Europe when the Byzantine Emperor, Michael the Stammerer, sent copies of some of them to the French King, Louis the Pious. From that time on their influence increased, and was strongly apparent in the works of Albertus Magnus and St. Thomas Aquinas. Those who would more fully understand this system will find it beautifully set out in the cosmic poems of Dante and Milton. The cantos of these two poets can be understood only by those acquainted with the Neoplatonic system.

The Neoplatonists have been condemned for their speculations in magic and theurgy, but the criticisms have come from persons not in sympathy with the mystical tradition. The magic of the Alexandrian mystics was not a vulgar sorcery devoted to the conjuring up of evil spirits and demons. It was the magic of love and the power of the spirit over the ordinary works of man. Dante represents the hierarchies as throned upon the petals of a great rose, a symbol of love and beauty. In all of their philosophy the Neoplatonists emphasize the mystical devotion by which the human soul finds union with the rose of heaven.

Again the rose appears, this time crucified on the cross of the Rosicrucians, thus linking this society with the cult of mystical adoration. So deeply was Dante influenced by the power of symbols that he could not look upon a rose growing by the roadside without passing into a state of ecstasy. Some of the esoteric schools of Asia use the lotus to convey the same mystical symbolism, and it appears in the religious art of nearly all Oriental peoples.

The Troubadours

The name troubadour is now applied to persons of sentimental mind who compose trivial verse and songs for romantic purposes. Few realize the depth or importance of this movement which was such a force in the medieval period of European history. The word troubadour is derived from the Provencal verb trobar, which means to find. The followers of this cult belonged to the orders of The Quest. The society was not large, numbering only about four hundred important members. It flourished from the 12th to the 14th century, and was finally destroyed by the Church as heretical.

The Troubadours catered to the artistic whims of kings
and princes, and were allowed extraordinary privileges. To
all appearances they were strolling minstrels who composed
songs for a fee, and entertained at fetes and banquets. The
itinerant poet often traveled alone, but sometimes he was
accompanied by a jongleur who acted as servant, and filled
the gaps in his master's program.

The Troubadours were party to most of the secrets and
intrigues of the European courts. It was not uncommon for
them to step out of their roles as entertainers to take part in
learned discourses and political councils. They alone could
contradict the king, ridicule the nobles, and attack the policies
of their time. Like the court jester they were immune from
all punishment, and might behave as they pleased.

Behind their gaudy costumes and gilded lutes the Troubadours were dedicated to a serious purpose. They were weary
of a religion of sorrow and pain, and were resolved to bring
back the happy pagan days of song and laughter. They
were mystics determined to bring a religion of love to mankind. To them love was not merely a sentimental emotion,
but a power from God which could be perfected by art and
science. Bound together by secret oaths, sworn to the defense
and protection of each other, they preserved Neoplatonic
mysticism through the troublous times of the medieval period.

Possibly the minstrels received inspiration from the Sufi
mystics of Arabia, whose verdant and extravagant verse concealed a doctrine of strange austerity. Under an apparently
utterly sensuous symbolism these mystics of the Near East,
like Omar Khayyam, taught a pure and lofty idealism entirely
meaningless to the vulgar.

The most important literary relic of the Troubadours is
Roman de la Rose. The first part was written about A. D.

1230 by Guillaume de Lorris, and the poem was completed forty years later by Jean de Meung. By reading between the lines one may learn a great deal about the secret society of the singers. The order was divided into seven degrees, and those of the highest degrees were called the Masters of Love. The poem also described a castle surrounded by a sevenfold wall. The wall was covered with strange emblems and figures, and only those who could explain the symbols were admitted to the inner house. The brothers had secret signs of recognition, and their organization prepared the way for Masonic orders of the modern world.

The Troubadours were also called minstrels, and for a very special reason. The word means minister, and this indicates that the singers were the priests of a secret worship. There were secret lodges of the order which were called Courts of Love. These did not house frivolous or immoral assemblages, but were places of ceremony and initiation into the pagan Mysteries. It is also likely that broad political and cultural issues were debated in these courts.

When a Troubadour composed a song for some important occasion he always addressed it to a beautiful and mysterious lady, but he would never reveal the name of the mistress of his verses. If asked, he remained silent. If a minstrel were engaged by a proud nobleman who lacked the vocal equipment to serenade his sweetheart, a suitable song was composed on the spot. Apparently it praised the beauty and virtue of the damsel who listened behind the drapes of her window. Everyone was pleased, and the singer received a generous fee, but as one of the Troubadours, Hugo de Brunet, explained, "I pretend that my song is for a mortal woman, but it is nothing of the kind."

As the alchemists were addicted to the seeming madness of goldmaking, so the Troubadours liked to be considered absorbed in their mortal passions. In both cases it was protection, but the Troubadours did not succeed in deceiving the ecclesiastical courts and were finally destroyed by the Inquisition.

Like the Beatrice of Dante, the mistress of the Troubadours was the symbol of sacred love, and personified pure wisdom as did the Virgin Sophia. The symbolism was borrowed from the Gnostics, and many of the attributes of Sophia were later embodied in the character of the Virgin Mary.

This digression will help to show the power of Neoplatonism in the molding of our modern religious viewpoint. There is no real break in the descent of the mystical tradition from the Orphics to Ralph Waldo Emerson. The form is forever changing, but the spirit is always the same. Remove Neoplatonism from our present systems of religion and most of the beauty and dignity that we cherish will vanish.

The orders of Chivalry were courts of love and honor. The Grail cycle belongs to the same descent. The great operas Parsifal, Lohengrin, and Tannhauser, are dramatic presentations of Neoplatonic mysticism. While these stories are Christian in their treatment, they are pagan in their ideas.

Francis Bacon played his part in the Court of the Muses on Mt. Parnassus. He was grand master of the Singers of Sweet Songs. As Chancellor of Parnassus, he ruled over the invisible empire of the poets and dreamers who served the God Apollo. Let us examine into the symbolism of the invisible empire in terms of the old philosophy.

Each man has two lives; an outer life lived in the world of men, and an inner life hidden from the common sight. Outwardly we must conform to the derelictions of our day. We must ply our trades and carry on the business of our world. We must struggle against the unreasonable ambitions of other men, and accept with patience both praise and ridicule. To those who are sensitive and by nature gentle, the weight of worldliness is a heavy affliction to the spirit. So when opportunity affords we fly to solitude, seeking within ourselves that peace and quiet which does not exist in human society.

Each man has his secret garden like the Rose Garden of Saadi. In this garden grows the tree of the soul, bearing flowers of exquisite beauty. This garden of the inner life is an oasis of fulfillment in a desert of waiting.

Bacon once wrote an essay on gardens, which is sometimes referred to in works on horticulture. Few, however, have sensed the true message of this little article. The inner world is the philosophic empire, the abode of thoughts, dreams, and aspirations. Here there is no illusion of time; past, present, and future dwell together in peace. Plato and Aristotle, Pythagoras and Euclid, still walk with their disciples in the garden of the mind. Loving thoughts can conjure up their forms, and the modern disciple may sit quietly at the feet of ancient masters.

To become a ruler of the inner world a man must be loved, not feared. He must be respected, not hated. The highest office attainable to a human being is that of prince over the secret gardens of the wise. Is this inner garden merely an illusion, the product of wishful thinking? Or is it the reality in man trying to break through and transform the outer wilderness into the likeness of itself? Is beauty only a hope, and ugliness the fact? The mystics would say that beauty is the reality and ugliness is a dream, a nightmare of the spirit which must pass away. Philosophy has proved that while the outer living is full of contention, all men are much alike in their dreams. In this world of the spirit there is neither race nor nation, only a longing for peace according to the understanding of the seeker. The outer life of man may be dominated by tyrants who bind nations and races to their ambitions, but tyranny cannot reach into the secret garden. The body can be destroyed, but never the dream. The more man is afflicted, the stronger his mysticism becomes.

The fate of the Troubadours is closely linked with the series of persecutions that destroyed the Albigenses, a sect which secured its name from the town of Albi. The Albigenses were an offshoot of the heresy of Manes, whose teachings so deeply influenced the early life of St. Augustine. The Crusaders had brought Europe into contact with the religions and philosophies of Greece, Arabia, and the Far East. The result was a strong revival of Neoplatonic mysticism, which took on political coloring and made an open attack on the papacy. All these Neoplatonic movements were pronounced heretical by the Church, and finally led to the setting up, in May of the year 1163, of the machinery for the Holy Inquisition. In sober fact, the Inquisition was an attempt to stamp out Neoplatonism in Europe.

The Knights Templars

In the year 1118 nine valiant and Christian-spirited knights formed themselves into an association which was to combine the attributes of knighthood and priesthood. They elected Hugh de Payens as Grand Master to whom they swore obedience, and they dedicated their swords, their moral strength, and their worldly possessions to the defense of the mysteries of the Christian faith. Thus came into existence the most powerful of all the medieval mystical orders, the Militia Templi, or the Knights Templars.

In the beginning the order was dedicated to poverty, and the seal of the Templars was the figure of two knights riding on one horse. In a few years, however, the Templars drew about them the most powerful nobles of Europe, and their wealth was beyond estimation. They set up nine thousand commanderies or lodges. At last their wealth became so great that the Church combined with the bankrupt royal houses of Europe to destroy the order. On March 14th, 1314 Jacques Bernhard de Molay, the last Grand Master of the Temple, was burned at the stake after six years of imprisonment and torture. All the properties of the Temple were confiscated, and its temporal power completely suppressed.

The Templars were accused of being pagans, of worshiping strange gods, of practicing mystical rites, of taking part in magical ceremonies, and of being inclined to the heresy of Manes. This contamination resulted from their contact with Gnostic, Cabalistic, and Islamic secret societies in Palestine. Most of the attacks made upon the Templars were inspired simply by avarice, and their supposed addiction to the worship of demons was only an excuse to justify their persecution and extermination. The philosophy of the Temple was essentially a Neoplatonic emphasis upon religion as a spiritual experience within the life of the initiate, rather than dependence upon the dogma of the Church.

With the martyrdom of the Templars, the esoteric orders of the ancient world disappeared as public institutions. General Albert Pike has pointed out that the broken sword of the Templars became the dagger hidden under the cloak of the brotherhood of Vengeance. The philosophical orders retired into a condition of complete secrecy, and their activities were concealed in the fables of the alchemists, the later Hermetists, Rosicrucians, and Illuminati. But the golden chain was never broken, and it was the Order of Vengeance that brought about the American and French Revolutions; gradually destroyed the divine rights of kings, and set up religious tolerance and political democracy among the nations of the Western Hemisphere. Modern democracy is a direct result of Alexandrian Neoplatonism and its conflict with ecclesiastical authority.

The Second Cycle of the Platonic Descent

In Volume I of this work we outlined the descent of Orphic theology from Pythagoras to St. Augustine. This was the foundation. The mystical rites established in Greece by the Thracian bard, Orpheus, were to grow and unfold until they dominated the intellectual development of the Occidental world. Orpheus composed hymns to the Sovereign Good. He revealed the religion of ecstasy, and taught the power of the mystical experience. The mystical theology of Orpheus was scientifically and mathematically revealed by Pythagoras. It was shaped into a noble system of moral, ethical, and political philosophy by Plato and his legitimate successors. Through the labors of Aristotle it was clarified, and became the basis of modern intellectualism. The sublime pattern was for a second time revealed to mankind through the Neoplatonic restoration, where it took on the aspect of a universal wisdom by embracing the metaphysical systems of Asia. In this final form it was imposed upon the structure of the early Christian Church by St. Augustine.

In the present volume we trace the descent through scholasticism as represented by Albertus Magnus and St. Thomas Aquinas. With the collapse of the schoolmen the heritage passed on to the humanists, of which group Paracelsus is an example. The intellectual revolt in the modern world against the limitations of unproved theory is personified by its great leader, Francis Bacon. The growth of the intellectual world was paralleled by the unfolding of the mystical aspect of Neoplatonism through such men as Jakob Boehme and Emanuel Swedenborg. Bacon and Boehme outlined broad policies, and it remained for the most meticulous thinker Europe has ever produced, Immanuel Kant, to reveal in detail that which previously had been stated only in general terms.

Thus Neoplatonism passed through the long, hard winter of its beginning. Then came the springtime in the fair climate of Alexandria, followed by an arduous summer in the confusion of Europe's Middle Age and the early centuries of modern time. Autumn came at last in the quiet, green hills of New England. Here in kindly words and gentle thoughts Emerson summed up the transcendentalism of twenty-five centuries in little essays that all could understand and love.

Although much has been accomplished, there is still a great deal to be attained. Reason has yet to prove the way of faith. We must labor to the end that heart and mind will bear testimony together. The sciences even now remain aloof, worshiping in the temple of the mind, and seeking with thought to solve the mystery of life. And the philosophers are still wrangling among themselves, offering their discord as homage at the altar of Aristotle. Neat little churches with pointed spires and whitewashed picket fences are modest but adamant survivals of theology's vanishing empire. The confusion lingers, but it is tempered by experience, and age has worn away most of the belligerancy. Old habits persist, however, and the oldest habit in the world is the impulse to divide.

Division results in common ruin. We stand, like Faust in his laboratory surrounded by scientific equipment, learned books, and sacred relics, and we echo his complaint, "Here I stand with all my lore, a fool no wiser than before." Without understanding there can be no perfection for the works of man, and this understanding must come from within. Science, philosophy, and theology have one necessity in common—the mystical experience. Only the power of the spirit can transmute science into truth, philosophy into wisdom, and religion into enlightened faith. Man himself must become the answer to the questions that he asks.

Neoplatonism is the mystical art of becoming. It has been said that life is an eternal process of becoming, the end of which is beyond human comprehension. It is not the growth of our institutions but the growth of ourselves that is our hope for the future. Too long have we accepted the symbol for the fact. We have measured progress in terms of the conquest of externals, and as our sciences expand we weep, as Alexander the Great wept because he had no more worlds to conquer.

Every day we are confronted with the challenge of becoming. As the burden of the outer world grows heavier upon us we look about desperately in search of strength and refuge. If we are honest we will admit that the fault lies in ourselves. We are not big enough for our jobs; we must become stronger as individuals if we are to survive. We plot, plan, scheme, and evade, but the problems only grow. Likely enough we end in a panic, the result of our own inadequacy. We seek advice from others, only to learn that we cannot understand the advice of the wise, and the advice of the foolish tends to make things worse. The materialist is profoundly comforted by the hope that beyond the grave there is nothing but silence and oblivion. At last he will be in peace, even if he is not privileged to be aware of his own contentment.

Of what virtue then are learned pronouncements, important conferences, and those dignified gatherings where the unenlightened arrive at weighty decisions relating to the unknown and the unknowable? The victim is completely trapped. He is in a cage from which he can find no way of escape. He may define the cage as he wills; he may decorate its walls with pictures of far vistas to create the illusion of freedom; he may gild the bars to make the cage less drab, but he is still a prisoner pacing the narrow width of his cell.

The late Harry Houdini was an expert at picking locks and freeing himself from behind prison bars. He said that his most difficult experience was an attempt to escape from a cell, the door of which he thought was locked. He tried for hours to pick the combination, and then by accident he leaned against the door. To his surprise it opened by this simple pressure.

The prison cell in which man has locked himself by the limitations which he has imposed upon his own consciousness is very like the one which caused Houdini so many trying hours. We are held to our mortal state by our own fixed belief that there is no escape. Having accepted life as a prison we either batter ourselves to death against its bars or settle down to the scientific process of trying to pick the lock.

There is but one way out of our mortal prison and that is through the growth of our inner consciousness. We become free as we become wise. There can be no real wisdom apart from the mystical experience. By the development of our own spiritual content we outgrow our physical limitations and pass from a mortal condition to an immortal state of being. It is this door upward and inward that has never been locked. The only reason we cannot use this door is that we have denied its existence, and have refused to accept the challenge of self-improvement as the way to freedom.

Neoplatonism is the doctrine of the open door that leads into the secret empire of the sages. In the doctrines of Zen Buddhism this door is called the gateless gate. He who discovers its mystery learns that every wall is transformed by truth into an open door. In the end the real fact becomes apparent; the whole physical universe is itself an open door. There are no walls, no bars, and no limitations except the ignorance of man.

Ignorance is variously defined. It can be applied to the unlettered, the unskilled, and the uninformed, but it is especially applicable to the unenlightened. Buddha applied the term ignorant to any person, schooled or unschooled, who was not aware of the spiritual mystery at the root of life. To believe that the conquest of the world can be achieved without the conquest of self is to be in a state of abysmal benightedness. Such a standard of estimation would work a serious hardship on the egos of modern intellectuals.

Faith cannot come from a mere desire to believe. It must arise from some inner conviction about God, nature, or man. This conviction must in turn originate in some extension of vision by which the larger aspect of living is experienced.

This is why the sorrows and misfortunes of our days have a tendency to enrich our consciousness. In adversity we become thoughtful; we search within ourselves for strength, and sometimes we find the door.

The Neoplatonic doctrine that the perfection of the mind leads naturally to illumination is the final reconciler of reason and faith. A disciplined faith built upward by ordered thinking is very different from the blind faith which afflicts theology. It is not a problem of rejecting values in the cause of spiritual consciousness. It is a perfectly natural unfoldment in the sphere of values in which superiors take their proper places over inferiors. In this way all conflict in the personality ceases, and consciousness becomes the proper ruler of the personality pattern.

The lofty idealism of such a mystical philosophy has contributed to beauty in every department of human endeavor. It has inspired the arts, enriched literature and poetry, and added luster to the learned professions. No one is better for being a materialist. No one is stronger because of unbelief. The work of the world, the progress in all departments of our social order, is the result of practical idealism. Great men always believe in something greater than themselves. By this belief they are inspired to overcome those obstacles which are always cast in the way of greatness.

Neoplatonic mysticism invites the thoughtful soul to share in the dream that has made man nobler than the brutes. Beyond the present horizon of our purpose lies the world of the Heroes. This is the empire of those who have found in themselves and through themselves the blessed natures of the gods.

How can we close the present chapter more appropriately than to quote once more from Plotinus? These are his words of counsel to those who seek wisdom: "The wise man recognizes the idea of the good within him. This he develops by withdrawal into the holy place of his own soul. He who does not understand how the soul contains the beautiful within itself seeks to realize beauty without by laborious production. His aim should be to concentrate and simplify, and so to expand his being, instead of going out into the manifold, to forsake it for the One, and so to float upward toward the divine font of being whose stream flows within him."

St. Thomas Aquinas

2

SCHOLASTICISM

Saint Thomas Aquinas

OUT of the myth and legend and general historical obscurity of the medieval world emerges the diminutive form of Albertus Magnus, Count von Bollstadt. In a time when philosophy, theology, and science were hopelessly confused it was difficult, if not impossible, to examine the achievements of an individual with anything resembling modern criticism. Nor do we possess much factual information about Albertus Magnus. In his own time he was called *The Ape of Aristotle* by his detractors. Those who saw no fault in him referred to him as *Doctor Universalis* and *Albert the Great*.

The physical proportions of Friar Albertus may be gathered from an incident recorded by Bullart. While in Rome Albertus kissed the feet of His Holiness the Pope. After the ceremony the Pope commanded him to rise, not realizing that Albertus was already standing upright. This would seem to justify the remark of one of the older historians that "Our Albertus was a very little man." But the intellect of Albertus exceeded the proportions of his body, for he was one of the most learned men of all time.

41

In an age when intellect was regarded as supernatural it was inevitable that Albertus should be accused of dabbling with infernal arts. His name has been associated with alchemy, magic, astrology, and cabala. A number of tracts have been attributed to him on very flimsy evidence. Most of them were catchpenny forgeries exploiting the venerable name of a famous man. One of these small books dealing with novel and unusual suggestions for midwives did little to further his reputation in the field of sober scholarship.

In view of the temper of the time it is quite probable that Albertus Magnus was interested in what we now glibly call the pseudo-sciences. All medieval chemistry was involved in Egyptian and Arabian alchemical speculation. It has been said that Albertus manufactured the gold to pay off the debts of his bishopric at Ratisbon, amassing this considerable sum by two years of diligent work with his retorts. Several alchemical writers include his name in the lists of their patron saints.

It was the same concerning astrology; the greatest professors of the old universities confused astrology with astronomy, teaching the latter principally for the sake of the former. Astrologers were men of consequence, and prospered unless their predictions failed or their findings ran contrary to the ambitions of their princes. A man with the learning of Albertus would most certainly be informed in the prevailing knowledge of his time. To discount his contribution to science and philosophy because of his unorthodox beliefs would be as foolish as to disparage Galileo and Copernicus because both of them cast horoscopes.

There is some dispute as to whether or not Albertus Magnus was one of the inventors of gunpowder. Here again the evidence is inadequate, but he lived in a time when men's minds were emerging from the limitations of the Dark Ages. New ideas were in order, and he contributed his share to the forward motion of his intellectual world.

Albertus Magnus, Doctor Universalis

Albertus Magnus was born at Lauingen in Swabia between 1193 and 1206. Although he came of good family and carried the title of count, he does not seem to have inherited any mental genius with his estates. As a young man he was slow of mind and dull of wit. He despaired of ever becoming learned, and his professors shared his despondency. His memory was especially bad, a particular misfortune in a time when all learning was nothing more than the capacity to remember. As a boy he showed marked religious leanings, but his adventures at the University of Padua merely discouraged him. How could a man with faulty faculties hope to master the profundities of Aristotelian logic and rhetoric?

In his extremity young Albertus turned to prayer for guidance. In one of his vigils the Virgin Mary appeared to him and promised her aid. Immediately an extraordinary intellectual vitality was manifested. His memory became prodigious, his reasoning powers gained an amazing acuteness, and he was transformed from a dullard into a mental giant. This is the legend, and in an age of miracles something remarkable certainly did occur.

Albertus Magnus emerged from mediocrity to become a leader of human thought. Profoundly grateful for the miracle that had so completely changed his life he took holy orders, and about 1223 became a Dominican and studied theology under the rules of the order at Bologna. He taught at Hildesheim, Freiburg, Ratisbon, Strasbourg, and Cologne, and the University of Paris made him Doctor of Theology in 1245. As a teacher and lecturer he gained a wide sphere of influence, and became bishop of Ratisbon in 1260, which bishopric he held for two years. At the command of the Pope he traveled through Germany and Bohemia preaching the eighth crusade, and undertaking various other ecclesiastical missions in Wurzburg and Strasbourg. The last ten years of his life were spent at Cologne in scholarly and scientific pursuits, notably in preparing commentaries on Aristotle and making the attempt to unite theology and Aristotelianism. He died on November 15th, 1280.

We read that in his closing years Albertus Magnus lost his intellectual powers, returning again to the dullness of wit that had been his prior to the vision of the Madonna. It is more probable that he was senile, but in those days natural causes were seldom considered if miraculous circumstances could be made to fit the occasion.

Father Theophilus defends the memory of Albertus from the stigma of sorcery by stating that God revealed the sanctity of this good man by several miraculous works and by preserving his body uncorrupted for a long time. He was beatified in 1622, named Doctor of the Church, and canonized by Pius XI in 1932. In 1480 the Great Chronicle of Belgium described him as *Magnus in Magia, Major in Philosophia, Maximus in Theologia,* thus summarizing the esteem in which he was held during the middle ages.

It is difficult to attempt an estimate of the personality of the great Albertus. To depart from the narrow path of historical certainties is to fall immediately into the abyss of legend. In fact the most interesting circumstance of his life is subject to this criticism, yet so persistent is the account that it seems advisable to include it here.

Albertus Magnus devoted thirty years of his life to the construction of an artificial being. Gabriel Naude in his *Apologie des Grandes Hommes* describes the making of this homunculus: "He had composed an entire man after this manner ... forming him under different aspects and constellations, the eyes for example ... when the sun was in the sign of the zodiac which answered to such a part, which he founded of metals mixed together, and marked with characters of the same signs and planets, and of their different and necessary aspects. And so the head, neck, shoulders, thighs, and legs, fashioned at different times and mounted and fastened together in the form of a man."

Naude called this figure the android, and by this name it is still known. It is a mistake, however, to assume that Albertus Magnus applied this name to the figure. Other early writers have suggested that the android was not made of metal but of artificial flesh and bones created by alchemical and magical means. There has been controversy as to whether or not the android was an instrument through which the devil could speak. The high level of scholastic thinking is well-represented in the decision arrived at by the schoolmen. They reason thus: As the devil is possessed of extraordinary powers it would be unnecessary for him to make use of a mechanical device; therefore it is judged that Albertus bound to his machine some poor, wandering ghost that prattled meaningless words.

It is further reported on the authority of several writers that the incessant babbling of the android interfered with the scholarly meditations of Albertus' favorite pupil, the immortal Saint Thomas Aquinas, who in a moment of irritation destroyed the mechanism. The fact that Saint Thomas himself does not refer to the incident is held as evidence that the entire account is a fable. It is possible that these several accounts were fathered upon Albertus by medieval historians.

Roger Bacon, the Franciscan monk and English mystical philosopher of the 13th century, is reported to have constructed a brazen talking head.

But it is Albertus Magnus, *Major in Philosophia,* who is our principal consideration. With him was ushered in the third period of scholastic philosophy, the systems of thinking that dominated the intellectual life of Europe from the 9th century to the Reformation, and survive even to our day in a modified form.

Charlemagne, (742-814) king of the Franks and emperor of the West, was a distinguished patron of learning. During his reign he created a system of cloister schools for the teaching of the seven liberal arts. These arts were divided into two groups: the *trivium,* composed of grammar, logic, and rhetoric, and the *quadrivium* which included arithmetic, geometry, music, and astronomy. Naturally, the cloister schools approached all knowledge from the inclusive viewpoint of theology, and they were immediately confronted with the problem of reconciling sacred and profane doctrines.

The teachers of the cloister schools were called *doctores scholastici,* and as their opinions took form and assumed the proportions of complete intellectualism the system was called *scholasticism.*

It has been said that there was no philosophy during the middle ages—only logic and theology. This is not correct, for the term theology included the entire field which has since been specialized into both philosophy and theology. It was the desire of Charlemagne to revive the broad principles of learning which had perished from the popular mind with the closing of the schools at Athens. He had recourse to the Aristotelian technique because Aristotle's systematic way of thinking seemed especially attractive at a time when all system was lacking. In Volume I of Journey in Truth we pointed out the Aristotelian fallacy, and the scholastics are a perfect example of this fallacy in action.

We are now inclined to picture the scholastics as Francis Bacon pictured them—hooded and robed intellectuals picking at the bones of the Aristotelian hen. When they had picked all the meat from the fowl they settled down to the process of gnawing the bones. It might be more fair to approach the subject in the words of Noire in his *Historical Introduction to Max Muller's Kant*. "Anyone who surveys with comprehensive gaze the development of philosophy as the thought of the world in its relation to mankind will see in the tranquil intellectual industry of the middle ages a great and significant mental crisis, an important and indispensable link between ancient and modern philosophy."

It was Albertus Magnus who first systematized the Neo-Aristotelianism of his time, and adapted it to the dogma of the prevailing church. To accomplish this huge task he had constant recourse to the Arabian commentators through whom the Greek tradition was largely preserved for Europe. The Arabs were romanticists in learning, and had considerably modified the intellectual austerity of the Greek thinkers. This simplified the work of Albertus; in fact it made the adaptation of Greek thought to Christian theology possible. He laid the foundation, but it remained for Saint Thomas Aquinas to perfect his master's labors. It is still a question as to which of the two, Albertus or Thomas, possessed the stronger intellect. But it is obvious that Thomas was the more subtle.

Thomas of Aquino, Doctor Angelicus

Thomas of Aquino, often called the *Doctor Angelicus,* the most celebrated of all the scholastic philosophers, was born in Italy about the year 1225 at the castle of his father, Count of Aquino, in the province of Naples. He was intended for a brilliant career in the secular world, and the circumstances of his birth assured him wealth and distinction. Early in life he came under the influence of the new Dominican order, the Friars Preachers. Their hold upon his mind increased with the years because he was by nature studious and the church was the principal repository of learning

Thomas received his early education from the monks of Monte Cassino, and later studied at the University of Naples. His intellect was especially suited for the subtleties of logic, and as his knowledge increased his resolution grew with it and he secretly entered the society of Friars Preachers when he was seventeen years old.

The Aquino family was by no means pleased at the prospect of their son exchanging his wealth for a monk's habit, and they made every possible effort to discourage his religious aspirations. His mother especially was indignant, and did all within her power to change his purpose. At the request of Thomas the Friars transferred him from one place to another to escape his mother's influence, but she followed him even to Rome. Although she lived in each city where he resided she was never permitted to see him. At last in desperation she conspired with his two elder brothers to abduct him by force. They waylaid him while he was on the road to Paris to complete his education, and carried him to the castle at Rocca Secca where they confined him for two years in the hope of persuading him to give up holy orders. He finally escaped through an upper window of the castle. This appears to have been the end of the family opposition, and young Thomas was permitted to engage in those pursuits which attained for him the name Angelic Doctor.

In Paris Thomas met and became a pupil of Albertus Magnus, and in 1245 when Albertus was called to Cologne Thomas went with him and remained his student for several years. Returning to Paris he gained a great reputation as a teacher, and as a leader of the Dominicans and the Friars in general when the Franciscans and the seculars stirred up trouble at the university. On the one hand was religion with its emphasis on the spiritual and intuitional faculties of the mind, and on the other was secular learning which emphasized the physical phenomena of life. The challenge offered by this conflict established Aquinas in his life work. He must prove that the two viewpoints could be reconciled. He was resolved to justify his concept by an elaborate use of logic.

Scholasticism has been accused of thinking from instead of toward a conclusion, and Aquinas is a brilliant example of this policy. Needless to say, a large part of modern thinking uses the same formula. Having decided what we wish to believe we cheerfully distort all facts until they prove our belief.

It is said that the most important conception which scholasticism originated was the conception of the concept itself. A concept is an intellectual object born of the mind but occupying an important relation to reality. To mature a concept or general idea and then bind the fact to the concept was the principal mental exercise of scholasticism.

Faith and Revelation

The philosophical and theological doctrines of Thomas Aquinas are called Thomism. His system is basically Aristotelian modified by the Arabian commentators and partly digested by Albertus Magnus. The principal tenet is the concept that faith is an extension of reason and that no conflict exists between the two. The mind, ascending through the various orders of learning comes finally to the contemplation of spiritual mysteries. These cannot be known by the intellect, but they can be discovered by faith. By faith man can approach God in the same way that by reason he can approach nature. Reason leads to philosophy, faith leads to revelation, and no inharmony exists between the two processes.

The examination of nature by the reasoning powers of the mind was Aristotle's forte. Nor is it easy to wander far afield when continually in the presence of physical facts. If we stray in our effort to explain the intangibles behind these facts, the facts themselves endure to refute our errors. As a result of the inevitable limitations imposed by visible things upon our impulse toward abstraction, reason tends toward materialism. A materialist is a person who hangs his faith on that which is demonstrable to the senses and the objective parts of the intellect.

But it is not so simple to attempt the organization and classification of imponderables. To reason accurately about things invisible and in themselves unknowable or unknown requires faculties not yet perfected in man. Things that are logically true may not be so in fact. It is hazardous to build an elaborate superstructure upon a hypothesis. This was the dilemma of the scholastics. Only partly informed about the physical world and its laws, they attempted to set up and demonstrate a dogmatic concept about the invisible world and its laws. They built on what they assumed to be the infallible foundation of Christian doctrine.

Let us parallel their endeavors with a similar attempt on the part of the Brahmans in India. It is said that these wise old Orientals examined and charted all space, physical and spiritual, extending their efforts a full ten inches beyond the circumference of eternity. However, the Brahmans did not approach the problem in the same way as did the Thomists. They had no intention of depending upon the frail instrument of faith. They set to work to perfect within the human being a group of extrasensory perceptions which would sustain their researches into abstraction. They believed that man had faculties within his mind which could be scientifically trained to cope with the mysteries of the spiritual world. This is the very essence of the doctrines of Yoga and Tantra.

Like most Aristotelians, the Thomists neglected to apply their scientific approach when fitting the individual for the task of metaphysical exploration. They trusted their weight to an intangible and inconstant factor which they called revelation. Like most mystics, they were so overwhelmed by the magnitude of Deity that they failed to approach God as a scientific problem.

We must not blame the scholastics too greatly for their mistakes. They lived in a time when a truly liberal attitude was impossible. They had neither the power nor the inclination to resist the pressure of ecclesiastical tradition. They made a valiant effort, and all European civilization has benefited by their endeavors, but they could not attain their principal end because they lacked the means.

In the consciousness of Thomas Aquinas there appears a strange conflict between the methods of Aristotle and Plato. This good churchman was attempting to accomplish a Platonic end by an Aristotelian technique. He wished to reconcile two widely divergent concepts by a common denominator. This was good Platonism and reveals the high measure of idealism which motivated Thomas's actions. But the Aristotelian instrument was faulty. It is hard to find the unity in things by a process of systematic separation.

We cannot analyze revelation by a method appropriate to the dissection of a plant. When we attempt to bind immortal truths to the limitations of the mortal mind something is lost, and the thing that is lost is truth itself. A systematized theology is not a link between man and his spirit. Man himself and not his dogma is the link with God. But this was contrary to theology, and therefore Aquinas could not perfect such a doctrine without destroying himself.

We have already mentioned that Albertus Magnus was touched, but not too deeply, by the stigma of sorcery. Thomas Aquinas also was reputed to be a magician, alchemist, and astrologer, and likewise with him these doubts were boldly raised and hotly contested. From all reports he was a lover of silence and solitude. He had weighty matters to ponder, and resented interruptions. The room in which he studied overlooked a thoroughfare where grooms were constantly exercising horses. This din so annoyed the good Thomas that he turned to magic as a remedy for the nuisance. He made a small horse of brass by means which he had learned from Albertus, and buried it three feet underground in the midst of the road. Thereafter no horse would pass that way. The grooms beat and spurred their animals, but to no avail, and finally chose another street in which to exercise their animals.

There is a persistent rumor that Albertus Magnus conveyed to his favorite disciple the secret of the philosophers' stone and the mystery of the universal medicine. There is no proof of this, but there are indications that Thomas was informed in chemistry. He is supposed to have first employed the word amalgam to signify an alloy of mercury with some other metal or metals. Probably most of the alchemical tracts attributed to him are forgeries.

Our particular purpose is to indicate the place of Thomas Aquinas in the descent of the Platonic tradition. We may be severely criticized for pointing out that in spite of his Aristotelian method he was at heart a Platonist, as to a degree was Aristotle himself. Both were touched by the lofty idealism of the Platonic vision. Aristotle was the victim of his own mind, and Aquinas was the victim of the one mind of his time—the Church.

The Greek theology as derived from the Orphics was a magnificent pageantry of gods and heroes administering world affairs from the lofty throne of Olympus. This vision was highly acceptable to the human mind, and when philosophically interpreted was satisfactory to the needs of both faith and reason. Plato was an Orphic, and his mystical convictions formed an adequate foundation for his material philosophy.

This happy state of things was lost, for the early Church and the early centuries of scholasticism brought little comfort. The human mind is addicted to a desire for facts, and possesses the will to acquire them. The learned are not of the mood for blind acceptance. The Church had to meet this challenge, and it was especially weak in what may be called system.

Christianity of itself is without cosmogenesis, anthropogenesis, or psychogenesis. It is a moral code, a way of living, but not an explanation of life. The Old Testament of the Jews was incorporated to supply part of this defect. From it the Church derived its cosmogenesis and part of its anthropogenesis. But this attempt toward solution only increased the difficulties. Actually the Old Testament is by no extension of the imagination a Christian book. It teaches an entirely different system of theology, and cannot be reconciled except by an elaborate process of interpretation.

Early Christianity had to cope with a well-organized pagan cosmos. It was the urge to compete in this respect which led the Venerable Bede to cry out against the pagan constellations moving in a majestic course over a Christian world. He assigned Jewish and Christian names to all the star groups to remedy the unfortunate condition, but his reforms found no lasting favor and the pagan heavens endured.

Jewish anthropogenesis did not help a great deal. The legend of Adam's rib required a great deal of explanation to render it acceptable. As for psychogenesis, it had no place at all. The Christian concept of the human soul was entirely contrary to the old Jewish doctrines. The Church could scarcely afford to borrow openly from the pagan systems which it had condemned wholeheartedly, but fortunately the early Fathers left ajar two doors that opened into paganism. They had a kindly word for the Egyptian hermetists and the immortal Hermes Trismegistus. They also were disposed to a friendliness for Plato and Aristotle, and through them the Greek schools.

Scholasticism was built upon these two foundations, the stones of which were held together with Arabian cement. The tragedy resulting from the closing of the Greek schools by the zealous Justinian was too apparent to be ignored. Paganism had left an aching void, and Islam threatened to fill it. This was a double crisis, and the Church knew that it must meet the challenge or perish. This does not infer that the Fathers reasoned this through; circumstances set up the pattern, and drastic remedies were indicated.

It is a pity that we do not possess a better record of the working of the medieval mind, but from slight indications we can infer the processes from the effects. Charlemagne resolved that facts should not perish in a sea of doubts, and set up the machinery for the re-establishment of philosophical order in the world. When we build we must have recourse to some plan. This the Church did not have, so Plato and Aristotle were drafted to meet the emergency.

Philosophy was reborn under the long shadow of the Church steeple. Wisdom has always been the reconciler of differences, and there were ample opportunities for such reconciliation. The universities, if we may apply so dignified a term to the schools of that day, had imbibed of Roman eclecticism. They took the attitude that learning was their province, and all who trespassed on their domain were thieves and robbers. They were still suffering the results of the division between the temple and the sciences which took place in Greece at the time of Hippocrates. There was no room in the vaulted passageways of the sciences for meddling priests with their notions about the trinity.

It appears that in the beginning theology attempted to ignore the sciences out of existence. Foolish men could bother themselves about nature and teeth and comets. The churchmen had no time for such vagaries; the human soul absorbed their entire attention. If they had any spare moments these could be spent in pondering the sermons of the early Fathers. In the end theology and the university became armed camps, each forever throwing verbal bludgeons at the other.

We are in much the same condition today. The universities on the one hand and the churches on the other have found no common denominator. The modern world is more tolerant, but this mental generosity does not indicate that the problem has been solved. Reason and revelation remain as two unreconciled methods for the accomplishment of the same end.

As through a glass darkly, Thomas Aquinas saw the thing that had to be done if Western civilization were to survive. Knowledge must be unified, and his basic pattern for solution was comparatively simple. By the union of philosophy and religion, theology came into being as a science, derived from the principles of a higher divine and spiritual science. Alchemically, theology was to be the universal solvent, a mystical mercury which could hold within itself the spirits of the other metals. In this way Aquinas set about to secure the temporal power of the Church in the intellectual world.

The Jarring Sects

Unfortunately, the scholastics themselves could not agree even on fundamentals. The Albertists differed from the Thomists in a number of particulars. The Scotists (followers of John Duns Scotus, the Doctor Subtilis) in turn rejected the mystical speculations of Bonaventura. Although by nature a Platonist devoted to mysticism, Bonaventura attacked the English philosopher, Roger Bacon, on the general grounds

that Bacon's scientific activities exceeded the bounds of orthodoxy. From such circumstances as these it will be readily
understood that scholasticism attempting to bind up the
wounds of division had a number of its own to bandage.

Bonaventura struggled valiantly with the problem of individualism and free will. In the end he took the ground that
the supreme good is union with Deity, and emerged as a
Christian Yogi. Finding little comfort in scholastic argument he abandoned himself entirely to mysticism as the only
possible solution to the difficulty.

Although both Albertus Magnus and Thomas Aquinas
derived much of their authority from Aristotle, they differed
from this old peripatetic on a number of theological points.
For example, Aristotle taught the eternity of the world as a
panacea for Plato's doctrine of regressive evasions. In other
words, Aristotle solved the problem of how the world began
by the simple expedient of assuming that the world had
always existed. With the book of Genesis hanging over their
heads, Magnus and Aquinas decided that the world had a
beginning in time. This they simplified by stating that time
had its beginning with the creation of the world. Here is
another form of the hen and egg dilemma. Magnus maintained that the creation by miraculous means could be ra-
tionally demonstrated, but recommended that the concept be
accepted as an article of faith rather than fact.

The Thomist scholastics ventured into the boldest of their
speculations. They attempted to solve the mystery of human
individuality by setting up matter as the cause of personality
differences and inequalities. Individuality was the result of
the mergence of the spiritual nature with the material principle. According to Magnus, "The variety of individuals depends entirely upon the division of matter." Here the scho-

lastics were attempting to build their bridge between Plato and Aristotle; between revelation and reason. Spiritual unity was an appropriate theological concept, and material division was an obvious natural fact.

The Scotists were quick to notice the weakness of the system advanced by Magnus and Aquinas. Their simple question, "What causes the division in matter?" confounded the elders. As all morality and immorality was intimately related to individuality, it was important to discover what was to blame for the diversity of human conduct and why it was so eccentric that it required salvation.

The argument took on added complexity when the angels were drawn in as an example of supermaterial individuality. There was common agreement as to the existence of angels, but certainly they were not corporeal beings; hence it followed that incorporeal beings could possess individuality. There was a difference in species which was superior to the difference in individuals; therefore each angel must be a separate species.

But men's opinions live on to plague them, and no sooner had the angelic world been put in order than the difficulty took a more imminent turn. If individuality is due to the descent of spirit into matter, does it not reasonably follow that the separation of spirit and matter at death extinguishes the individuality? As the immortality of man is a cardinal tenet of faith, the Thomists were on the horns of a dilemma. Their solution was to include in the soul unit the power to endure as an immaterial form. God created the soul superior to the body and capable of surviving the dissolution of the body. Thus the human being consisted of two natures, a spiritual individuality derived from God, and a material individuality resulting from its union with matter.

It will thus be seen that the principal end of scholasticism was neither attained nor attainable according to their system. Striving ever to unite, they invariably arrived at division. Seeking to prove the unity of the soul, they were obliged finally to accept its twofold structure. This fulfills the purpose of reason, which requires contrast for its very survival. The only hope was revelation, the inward spiritual realization of a unity which could not be demonstrated by the intellect.

One other example will show the magnitude of the task which the scholastics had set for themselves. It is concerned with the nature of good. Aquinas asserted that God commands what is good because it is good. This assumed the sovereignty of good, with Deity administering that sovereignty by virtue of participation in its substance. Thus good comes first, and God comes second. The Scotists hotly contested this point. According to them, that which is good is only good because God so wills that it shall be. By this viewpoint God comes first, and his will establishes the absolute standard of good to which all creatures must conform. Or must they conform? Aquinas taught a moderate determinism; the human will is under the dominion of the reason by which it is impelled toward right action. Yet obviously it is quite possible for the human being to perform actions that are not good. The Scotists pointed this out and decided that the will could act as it pleased. In this respect it appears that they found solid ground. Aquinas therefore decided that both God and man possessed the power to select good, and the will to conform to the pattern of universal integrity. In other words Aquinas, having trouble with his Aristotelianism, took refuge in Platonism.

By the time the jarring sects had each contributed its own confusion to the general uncertainty, scholasticism was breaking up and breaking down. The Thomists and the Scotists divided the philosophic universe among themselves and set up their several kingdoms in the intellectual abyss. Their problem was too large for their time, and six hundred years later it is still too large. There were too many hypotheses and not enough facts. The mind cannot think in a straight line if it has been conditioned to think in curves. The scholastics were permitted to function only within the narrow enclosure of Christian doctrine. They were defeated from the first, but struggled valiantly against inevitables.

In the 14th century William of Ockham, the Invincible Doctor, assayed the role of a philosophic Sampson in wrecking the temple of the theological Philistines. He regarded the arguments about the substance of individuality as absurd. The individual was the one reality requiring no explanation but a vast amount of understanding. It was the duty and privilege of the individual to be the one certainty in an uncertain life. It was not up to universals to explain individuals; it was up to individuals to explain universals. There is much in the doctrines of Ockham reminiscent of the pragmatism of William James of Harvard, the dean of American thinkers. The world becomes what the individual believes it to be, wills it to be, and causes it to be by action.

The Principal Teachings of St. Thomas Aquinas

It has been stated that the principal doctrine of Saint Thomas can be summed up as "The absence of any formal distinction between the domain of philosophy and that of theology." This is a solid Neoplatonic foundation; in fact, the most important of the Greek mystical tenets. Knowledge is an extension upward toward the substance of truth, and the process of knowing is a gradual ascent of the power to know through the various levels or degrees of a single spiritual substance. The material world is an extension of God downward. The spiritual world is an extension of nature upward. There is no formal distinction between spirit and matter, as they are conditions of one essence. In the intellectual world, therefore, there can be no formal distinction between sacred and profane knowledge. All knowledge is in substance spiritual and has material significance only through the accidents of extension. Upon this solid and philosophically irrefutable foundation of Neoplatonic theurgy the doctrines of Thomism found their essential footings.

The Church of St. Catarina at Pisa enshrines an important painting representing Saint Thomas Aquinas. He is shown with his *Summa contra Gentiles* upon his lap, and he is surrounded by figures of saints and great Biblical teachers. To his right stands Aristotle holding up his *Ethics,* and to his left is Plato with the *Timaeus.* From these proceed rays which reach to the ears of the saint. It would scarcely be possible to symbolize more completely the relationship between the philosophy of Saint Thomas and the classical school of Greece.

It is generally acknowledged that Aquinas was profoundly influenced by Aristotle, and his followers have been accused of being so addicted to the peripatetic school as to accept large portions of the philosophy without question or examination. It is known that he was a student of the *Timaeus* of Plato, and he regrets that the *Republic* was not accessible in his time. There is still much debate as to the degree that Thomism was influenced by Neoplatonism.

In his work on logic Karl von Prantl says that Saint Thomas corrupted both Aristotelianism and Platonism by addicting

himself to the mysticism of the book *De Causis*. Saint
Thomas was well-aware of the fact that this book was by
Proclus, the last of the great Neoplatonists. He also drew
extensively from Boethius, Cicero, Macrobius, and Seneca.
Most of the masters quoted by him were to some degree influenced by the flow of North African Neoplatonic mystical
speculation.

That Saint Thomas was given to mystical and metaphysical disciplines is evidenced by one of the closing episodes of
his life. At the castle of Magenza, which belonged to one
of his nieces, he passed into a state of trance or ecstasy. This
endured for such a long time that it greatly enfeebled his
body and possibly hastened his death. There can be no doubt
that he was addicted to various mystical practices reminiscent
of the divine experiences recorded by the later Platonists.

The personal life of Aquinas was devoted almost entirely
to lecturing and writing. He refused the honors which the
Church wished to bestow because they interfered with the
principal activities of his life. He was offered the abbacy of
Monte Cassino, and the archbishopric of Naples. Death
came to him in 1274 after several weeks of illness at Fossa-
nuova Monastery near Sonnino, province of Rome. He was
only forty-nine when he died, predeceasing his master, Albertus Magnus, by six years.

Thomas Aquinas was canonized in 1323, and in 1888 he
was declared the patron saint of all Roman Catholic educational institutions. By any estimate he merited the honors
which have been conferred upon his memory. He was by far
the greatest intellect in the history of the Church. Building
upon the foundation laid by Saint Augustine, and extending
his mind to the consideration of every branch of learning,

he perfected the theological system so far as this was possible within a structure of conflicting beliefs.

Fortunately for Saint Thomas, he did not live to see the collapse of academic scholasticism. But all the works of man must perish, and the scholastics fell before the impact of the modern mind. The 15th century brought with it a new attitude toward life and its problems. Humanism was born. Man was emerging from the chaos of his own beliefs. Philosophy, religion, and science, were taking their places as the instruments of human accomplishment. Man was no longer to be the servant of learning. It was now time for learning to become the servant of human necessity. There was a difficult period of transition. The scholastics dominated all the institutions of learning, and they were resolved to hold the world mind to the traditional pattern. The schools became fortresses of dogma, and from these high and impregnable structures the scholastics sallied forth to do battle with the knights-errant of humanism. For a time Western civilization was locked in struggle, but in the end humanism won. It was progress toward solution, but not solution in itself. One kind of speculation was exchanged for another, but speculation continued. The humanists had an answer but not *the* answer. Conflict soon arose among them, and the old pattern was repeated on another plane of mind.

If the change broadened man's physical perspective it did so by narrowing and imprisoning his ideals. Philosophy broke entirely with Neoplatonic vision and mysticism. The effort to reconcile spirit and matter had failed, and materialism became the ruling passion. If the scholastics had gone off into vagaries concerning the number of angels who could dance at one time on the head of a pin, the humanists also had their foibles. They dedicated the human intellect to discover the number of atoms that composed the head of the pin. Each arrived at momentous conclusions, but human beings continued to be born, to suffer, and to die as before.

The struggle between theology and the sciences led to the persecution of such men as Galileo and Copernicus. The scholastics should not be overly condemned for their attitude, for it is shared by all human beings on subjects involving progress. We have substituted ridicule for persecution, but continue to regard with anxiety anything that is new or different from our traditional way. Edison, Bell, and Fulton all felt the weight of a popular scholastic attitude. When these inventors demonstrated their discoveries the spectators assembled not to applaud endeavor but to cheer for failure. A man who went to East Orange to see Edison's first experiments with the street car returned home angry and chagrined, announcing bitterly, "The darned thing ran!" If centuries of examples and proof beyond dispute of man's ability to perfect new devices has not tempered our scholastic tendencies, why should we condemn medieval thinkers who had a much more limited perspective?

From Charlemagne to the Reformation scholasticism was the only light that guided European thought. Its fault lay not in its vision but in its method. The early scholastics realized that in some mysterious way man's spiritual life was affected by his physical way of living. Millions of moderns have not yet grown up to this realization. The spiritual life of man is still ignored, and as a result few of his physical affairs go well.

The Advent of Humanism

With the advent of humanism mankind started off on a new tangent—the mastery of physical nature. Matter as an obstacle to the motion of life must be explained. Astrology lost its glamour and became sober astronomy. Alchemy divorced itself from hermetic speculations and took on the somber livery of a science. Metaphysics was swallowed up in physics. Mathematics lost its Pythagorean overtones to become the instrument for estimating profit and loss. The arts did not escape the general trend. Painting and sculpture departed from idealism to assume it to be true realism that the worst is the fact.

The will asserting itself manifested as an all-pervading willfulness. Man can accomplish anything that he wills to accomplish, and this concept invited a broad experimentalism. Forbidden previously to try anything new, the mind resolved to try everything new, substituting trial and error for dogma. We are still suffering from the consequences of this ill-guided enthusiasm. But progress is inevitable, and we learn from our mistakes.

With the rise of humanism open rebellion broke out among the lettered and the learned. The first attack was upon authority, and unfortunately most authority will not bear investigation. Humanism included the humanizing of the immortals. Great men of the past were suddenly revealed to be human after all. True, there are degrees of human-ness and some were more human than others, but all were subject to fallacy. Their findings were worthy of investiga-tion and consideration, but not of blind acceptance. This was a cataclysmic force in the intellectual world. No one had ever visualized Arsitotle as a small child cutting teeth. It had been assumed that he was born in the fullness of his glory, like Minerva from the head of Zeus. This prevailing skepticism about the omnipotence of mortals worked a special hardship on the Church. It raised the question as to the

infallibility of various doctrines which were definitely trace-
able to human origin. If Saint Ambrose could have been
wrong, if Saint Jerome could have erred, and if Saint Augustine could have been at fault in any detail, then the worst in
all things could be true. The theologians retired to their
scholastic strongholds and left the world to its follies.

If, however, the infallibility of the Church remained
(temporarily at least) unassailable, the fallibility in the secular parts of scholasticism offered a Roman holiday for the
humanists. Galen and Avicenna were tumbled from their
thrones, and many a noble ancient lost his following.

But it is one thing to tear down idols and quite another
thing to put great ideals in their places. It was fashionable
to disbelieve, but universal suspicion brings little comfort.
If Galen and Avicenna were wrong, who then was right?
The early Church had begun its career by a general attack
upon the pagans, and modern science started its illustrious
course with a wholehearted attack upon scholastic theology.

Something must be found to fill the void left by the rejec-
tion of tradition. To meet this a new technique was evolved
based upon observation and experimentation. Tradition
could not be entirely eliminated. To take away the past
would be to leave nothing. The past must be endured as a
necessary evil, but all tradition was to be subjected to the
censorship of present findings.

Observation came first because the human faculties were
readily available, but the means for controlled experimentation were limited. The result was the rise of observational-
ism. Knowledge was built up from the testimony of the
senses, presumably under the control of that attenuated faculty called common sense. The *grand tour* which had been
a part of medieval education was no longer a journey from

one scholastic institution to another. He who observed the most was the wisest, and whenever possible circumstances should be examined on their own ground. We like to think that this attitude resulted in the era of exploration which led to the discovery of the Western Hemisphere and other distant lands. A more truly humanistic attitude, however, is that exploration was inspired by cupidity rather than by the basic love of learning.

Scholars began to mingle, not in the vaulted universities but in the privacy of their own homes. Here they communicated to each other their reasonable doubts about the curriculum. Travelers from afar joined the circles and brought news of foreign progress. The change wrought in medicine was especially outstanding. The doctors exchanged favorite remedies and gained a reputation among their own kind for their individual efforts. All men need a certain amount of approbation in order to do their best work. As individual thinking became fashionable the intellectual level of the times rose correspondingly.

The early humanists revolted, not against the foundations of knowledge but against scholastic interpretation of source material. They maintained the right of the individual to arrive at his own conclusions in matters of belief and opinion. The humanism of Auguste Comte emphasizes the dignity of the human being and rejects the separate existence of a divine power. Deity is in man and working through man and is a part of humanity and nature. It does not necessarily follow that the humanists interpreted the indwelling divinity in terms of mysticism. It was their tendency to impersonalize God and regard so-called spiritual values as overtones of physical existence. Humanism prepared the way for modernism, and its rise resulted in a definite modification of religious doctrine.

The old belief that the earth was the footstool of God rapidly passed out of fashion. So far did the motion go that in the end the concept of Deity was tolerated as a necessary evil.

There were times in the course of humanism when Deity would have been eliminated completely had it not been for a delicate economic consideration. The universities depended upon popular support for their survival. God-fearing commoners could scarcely be expected to support godless institutions. The wiser course was a compromise between the two extremes. God was left outermost space for his abode, but was refused admission to the academic campus. This state of affairs endures with some modification to our present time.

The earlier humanists were neither atheists nor agnostics. They had no quarrel with God, but a strong case against the priestcraft in general. But once a ball starts to roll and gathers momentum it is difficult to predict the consequences. The humanist motion became an irresistible force sweeping away not only an elaborate structure of fallacies but at the same time undermining a good part of European idealism. Internal conflict was inevitable. Humanism could not be accepted by those of mystical inclinations. The transcendentalists revolted, and revived romanticism as a panacea for the adoration of sterile facts. The romanticists started a knight-errantry of their own, and most of them ended up like Don Quixote lancing windmills. Cervantes' story of Don Quixote is a satire on romanticism in general. It is the story of the impulse of the human mind to escape from the challenge of reality.

There is a streak of romanticism in the composition of every human being who has developed his mind sufficiently to manifest the power of imagination. The common tendency is to use a symbolical means of escaping present problems. Now is the time of stress. To escape stress we must depart from now into some other time. So often we hear people say, "If only I could have lived in ancient Greece!" or "If only I had been born in India!" Thus romanticism is a form of escape mechanism; a departure out of the darkness of personal responsibility into some promised land where the desired is a reality.

As long as human beings swing from one extreme to the other in their opinions, reality eludes them. The scholastics attempted to bind the mind to a preconception, and failed. The humanists created an opposite preconception, gathered an enthusiastic following, and likewise failed for lack of temperance. The romanticists offered a remedy that was as fatal as the ailment, and their failure likewise was inevitable. Thus the story of human thought comprises a long pageantry of failures, and the truth which has been sought by trial and error remains elusive.

3

NEOPLATONISTS OF THE RENAISSANCE

PHILIPPUS AUREOLUS PARACELSUS

THE fall of Constantinople brought about a momentous change in the intellectual life of Europe. The Byzantine scholars departed in haste from the City of the Golden Horn, bringing with them to western Europe the classical learning of ancient Greece. The invention of the printing press and the discovery of America also played an important part in the change. The foundation laid in the 14th and 15th centuries became the solid basis of the Renaissance.

In order to appreciate the 'great arising' we must examine the circumstances of the intellectual rebellion that cleared the way for our modern trend of life. The 15th century was an age of mental heroes. In every part of Europe champions of humanistic learning were locked in mortal combat with the votaries of scholasticism.

Trithemius of Sponheim

Consider the case of Johannes von Heidenberg, who was born in Trittenheim on the Moselle in 1462. As was the fashion of the time he adopted the name of his birthplace and is known to history as Johannes Tritheim (Latinized

Paracelsus

form Trithemius). He was the son of a vinedresser, and was only a year old when his father died. His mother married a second time, bringing a harsh and brutal stepfather into the small boy's life. The stepfather had no place for learning in his personality pattern, and Johannes had to learn reading and the rudiments of Latin secretly at night with the aid of a kindly neighbor.

Tritheim left home at an early age and went to Treves in search of an education. Later he attended Heidelberg, where he distinguished himself in literature. In 1482 while returning home for a visit he was stopped by a heavy snowstorm and took refuge in the monastery at Sponheim. He was received with such kindness by the monks that he decided to join the Benedictines and devote his life to scholarship. He must have possessed an exceptional mind, for three years later the twenty-three year old scholar was chosen abbot of the monastery.

At the time Tritheim became abbot of Sponheim the library consisted of less than forty volumes. He immediately set about to remedy this condition. He insisted that the monks employ themselves by making copies of important works and compiling new material. It appears that theretofore the monks had enjoyed much luxury and leisure, and they were far from pleased with the prospect of hard work. They grumbled along for twenty-three years under the watchful eye of the abbot, until the library contained hundreds of fine manuscripts. At last, while Tritheim was on a journey, the dissatisfied faction stirred up a riot in the monastery. Learning of the condition Johannes chose not to return, and was made abbot of the Scottish monastery of St. James at Wurzburg, where he died in peace and tranquillity eight years later.

Tritheim gained considerable reputation as a historian and theologian, but his historical writings are generally regarded as unreliable. He was known also as a alchemist, necromancer, and cabalist. Perhaps his greatest bid for fame was his research into ciphers and methods of secret writing. He invented a number of ciphers and codes, and rescued others from oblivion. A century later Augustus, Duke of Brunswick-Luneburg, using the pseudonym Gustavus Selenus, republished with considerable revision the work of Tritheim on ciphers, under the title *Cryptomenitices et Cryptographiae.* Part of the text of this work is still used by various governments in decoding secret documents.

We have in our library an early pen-and-ink sketch of Tritheim showing him to be a venerable, bearded gentleman wearing the gown and bonnet of a scholar. As he was the first known to have recorded the adventures of old Dr. Faust it seems safe to infer that the good abbot was interested in magic, although he violently protested his innocence of all sorcery.

Paracelsus, the Swiss Hermes

Theophrastus Bombastus von Hohenheim (Paracelsus) the link that connected Tritheim with the Neoplatonic descent, was born near Einsiedeln in Switzerland about 1491. He accumulated several additional names in the course of his wanderings, and at the height of his career liked to be called Philippus Aureolus Theophrastus Bombastus Paracelsus von Hohenheim. Historians were not of a mood to wrestle with such a title, and for centuries he has been known simply as Paracelsus. How he originally secured the name Paracelsus is a matter of dispute. Some say he took it to indicate that he regarded himself superior to the Roman physician Celsus, who gained a wide reputation during the reign of the Roman Emperor Augustus. Others hold that it was given by the young man's father because of early indications of genius. His father was a physician, though not outstanding, and his mother was for some years superintendent of the local hospital. With both of his parents engaged in the healing arts it was not surprising that he should devote his life to medicine.

Paracelsus first studied medicine with his father, from whom he learned all that was available in the form of therapeutic tradition. Physicians not only diagnosed and treated, but also prepared all of their own medications according to ability and Galen. There was no standard pharmacopoeia, and most of the materials obtainable were of inferior quality. Doctors had herb gardens in their own yards, and dumped into their prescriptions anything suspected of possessing medicinal virtue. Those who could not afford doctors were left to die of their diseases, and those who could afford them died of the remedies.

When Paracelsus was about sixteen he entered the university at Basel. Here his worst fears were realized. The scholastics were immersed in their own conceits; they were not only ignorant, but blissfully ignorant of their own ignorance. It was at Basel that Paracelsus broke from the traditional practice of medicine. Years later he described his youthful decision in these words: "I had in the beginning, just as much as my opponents, thrown myself with fervent zeal on the teachers; but when I saw that nothing resulted from their practice but killing, death, murdering, laming and distorting—that the greatest number of complaints were deemed by them incurable, and that they scarcely adminis-

tered anything but syrups, laxatives, purgatives, oatmeal
gruel, pumpkins, citrons, jalap, and other such messes, with
everlasting clysters, I determined to abandon such a miserable
art, and to seek truth by some other way."

Paracelsus was still in his later teens when the rumor
reached his ears that Tritheim was experimenting with
alchemy. He hastened to Sponheim and besought the learned
abbot to accept him as a pupil. An enduring friendship was
established that was to influence the entire course of modern
science. The profound knowledge of the Scriptures revealed
in the Paracelsian writings, and the spirit of mysticism
which pervades the philosophy of Paracelsus, can be traced
to his contact with Tritheim.

The good abbot was deep in alchemical formulas and the
long cycles of distillation and putrefaction which were the
traditional methods for the transmutation of metals. Paracelsus had not the patience for such procedures, and soon
tired of the monastic environment. It occurred to his fertile
mind that nature was the mother of the minerals, and that
a practical alchemist should have an intimate knowledge of
her ways.

He left Sponheim and went to Tirol where he worked in
the silver mines and laboratories of the Fuggers. There he
found the thing he sought; a direct contact with reality. He
talked with the miners and watched them as they extracted
the precious metals from the veins in the rock. He gained
a new estimation of the value of machinery, and witnessed
the accidents and misfortunes that plagued the art. He
studied the diseases that afflicted the workmen, and experi-
mented with mineral waters. By comparing the various text-
books on mining with the information he secured by direct
contact he realized that only those who mined understood

mining. He learned more by conversation with the un-lettered workmen who had labored for years in the earth than could be found in the texts of the most famous theo-retical scholars.

His experience in Tirol determined his future. He resolved to examine all arts and sciences firsthand. He would study only with those who really knew through experience. If the professors wished to sit apart in their fine robes and mumble theories, so much the worse for them; he would have no part in such a policy. Those who taught what they them-selves did not really know were worse than fools; they were rogues preying upon the ignorance of mankind.

For nine years Paracelsus wandered up and down the face of Europe seeking knowledge. He did not travel by post chaise as did the elegant men of letters, but chose to trudge the weary way on foot. He was a vagabond of science, always questioning, always observing, and ever mind-ful of local traditions and customs. "The beasts of the fields," he would say "know the laws and manners of their kind, yet they do not attend universities. They are instructed by God and nature. Should not men follow this example?"

Among the poor and the unschooled he discovered a world unknown to the proud scientists of his day. He be-came one with the forlorn and the forgotten. He spoke their language, lived their lives, and shared their confidences. He mingled with gypsies and witches, and frequented the hovels of the widows who dried herbs and wrought spells and enchantments. He found men who were branded ped-dlers and quacks more sincere and honest than the court physicians. The poor lived by common sense and their wits, but they lived, while the victims of the barbers died in droves.

Penniless most of the time, Paracelsus supported himself as best he could through the long years of his wanderings. He taught all who would listen, and augmented his means with astrology and other forms of divination. At one time he sold Bibles, and it is said that he could recite the Old Testament from memory, seldom failing in a single word. He was refused the association of doctors because he had the appearance of a beggar. Never overly neat about his person, his poverty reduced him to rags, but the very circumstance that alienated him from the rich endeared him to the poor. He was one of them; he understood them and they loved him.

There were brief interludes of prosperity, and on numerous occasions he could have established a profitable practice. But the love of learning forced him back to the dirt road that led to greater knowledge. The doctors were always his enemies, but it cannot be said that he made any serious efforts to win their friendship. He ridiculed them in public and cursed them in private. His arrogant spirit was never tempered by adversity, and the exasperated medics several times plotted his destruction.

It is difficult to estimate the character of a man whose activities have been chronicled principally by his detractors. They describe for us a person of violent temper, vicious tongue, and corrupt morals. He held the scientists of his day in utter contempt, and expressed his disgust with a total lack of social grace. It may be said of him that at least he was not inhibited.

Bombast by name and bombastic by nature, he gained a wide reputation for ill-breeding. From a more generous viewpoint one might say that he lived in a constant state of righteous indignation. And there were good grounds for his dispositional inclemency. Dr. Hemmann in his *Medico-Surgical Essays* describes Paracelsus as living in an age when the science of medicine had degenerated to shallow school gossip, and the disciples of Galen, in spite of their gossiping and their passion for controversy and disputation, were the most wretched pretenders in the healing of diseases. The Galenic doctors with their bleeding, purging, and emetics, were seldom successful in treating disease. Hemmann gives us much more in the same vein, and it is easy to understand that the contemporary medics might have interpreted the remarks as uncultured.

It is not often that nature produces a scientist or philosopher with a militant disposition, but Paracelsus was an exception to all rules, human and divine.

The name of Paracelsus would now be one of the most honored in all the world had he not been addicted to mysticism. Like Pythagoras he acknowledged the reality of magical forces and arts, and like Pythagoras his reputation has suffered accordingly. Even today, when we boast of mental liberality, metaphysical speculation is still the unforgivable sin in science. Modern apologists attempt to clear Paracelsus from the taint of hateful mysticism by explaining that he used the occult words only because no other terminology was available, but anyone familiar with the Paracelsian writings knows that this is only adding injustice to iniquity.

Paracelsus was certainly the most traveled physician of his time. In the course of his life he visited Italy, France, Denmark, Sweden, Prussia, Bohemia, Poland, Spain, England, and most of the Balkan countries. While in Russia he met a prince of the Tatars with whom he traveled to Constantinople. There is a legend that he reached India, but this is doubted by modern historians.

From the Mohammedan doctors he learned much that was useful and important in the field of medicine. Islam was the repository of learning, and he discovered among the Islamic scholars the true spirit of scientific inquiry. At last the wanderer had met his own kind, and this contact justified his entire philosophy of healing and set him more firmly in his course.

War broke out in the Netherlands while he was in England, and he immediately applied for the post of barber-surgeon in the Dutch army. His real motive was to perfect himself in practical surgery, about the only branch of the medical arts practiced in the army. Surgery in the 16th century was performed with incredible indifference to human suffering. Limbs were amputated with a crude saw, no anesthetic was used, and the stumps were cauterized with a red-hot iron. Most of the patients, or victims, died of shock or bled to death. According to the ethics of the time surgeons were not really doctors but were recruited from among the barbers, whose red and white striped pole was the symbol of the bleeding bandage.

Paracelsus was about thirty-two when he returned to Germany with a considerable reputation as a physician and surgeon. He was invited to lecture at the University of Basel. Shortly thereafter he was requested to take a professorship in physics, medicine, and surgery, and it appeared that he was on the road to academic success and fame. He professed to 'internal medicine' and began his instruction by burning the books of Galen and Avicenna in a brass pan after pouring sulphur and niter over them. By this and other startling innovations he so dumfounded the faculty of the university that for a short time it was speechless. In addition to his extraordinary pretensions he performed a number of local cures upon cases pronounced hopeless by the doctors.

Not only was Paracelsus remorseless in his attack on the physicians; he also turned his spleen toward the apothecaries, whom he accused of wilfully altering the prescriptions for their own profit. Many a respected medic suffered in his private practice, and the reputation of the new physician eclipsed that of the so-called respectable practitioner.

The masters of the university gradually recovered from the spell which Paracelsus had cast over them, and settled down to the systematic process of discrediting him whenever opportunity afforded. They first resorted to an ancient artifice by questioning his right to practice medicine without the usual permits and patents, which they made sure he could not obtain. This ruse failed because he merited so much public support that the doctors were afraid to show their hands. They finally resolved to adapt providence to their purposes.

A certain percentage of the sick and aged had no possibility of recovery. The doctors did all in their power to see that Paracelsus would inherit such cases. He was held responsible for every death that he attended. In some instances he accomplished what verged upon the miraculous, but his failures were given every possible publicity. His personality and temperament were also used against him. It was reported that he was in a constant state of intoxication even while teaching, but like the heroes of Rabelais he was sotted and cold sober at the same time. His slovenly appearance was termed unprofessional and his ethics unspeakable, but he remained the prince of physicians, the Swiss Hermes, the greatest healer of his time.

If the grievances due to his success were many, there was another fault equally unforgivable. He refused to deliver his lectures in Latin. This was a heresy that rocked the foundations of the sciences. His explanation was simple: "I have no desire to be elegant; I desire to be understood." It was enough to be confronted with the challenge of learning, and too much to be forced to explain the unexplainable in bastard Latin. Medieval, or bastard Latin as it is usually called, was a corruption of classical Latin so foul in its structural deformities that even modern scholars have difficulty in reading it. Paracelsus regarded this lingual catastrophe as eminently suitable to cover up ignorance but unfit for the simple statement of known facts.

But perhaps the principal reason for professional resentment was that he endeavored to make scientific knowledge available to the general public. He was one of the first to think in terms of medical knowledge as part of common education. He realized the need for hygiene and eugenics in the home. The people spoke Low German. The physician was their servant. Therefore let him speak their language and not mumble Latin phrases in his beard.

On one occasion Paracelsus assembled the professors to hear a learned discourse on fermentation. After they had gathered in solemn dignity he strutted out before them with a large covered dish. They probably suspected that the dish contained the philosophers' stone or some other equally incredible substance. But when he removed the lid they found that the dish contained only human excrement. This was the final straw! The entire assemblage rose and departed in high dudgeon. Paracelsus stood in the middle of the floor shouting after them: "You call yourselves doctors and yet you will not deign even to look upon feces, let alone examine it. Yet here, gentlemen, is to be found one of the greatest secrets of the diagnostic art."

A break was inevitable, and it came in a spectacular way as did everything in the life of Paracelsus. The canon Cornelius von Lichtenfels was stricken with an obscure ailment. The doctors gathered about him and opined variously. There were consultations, and the old books were dragged out to find what Galen recommended. But it seems that in this case the Galenic oracle was silent. The canon grew worse and worse, until at last his condition was pronounced hopeless. He had been purged and bled until body and soul could no longer stand the strain and were moved to dissolve partnership. But love of life is stronger even than prejudice, and in his extremity Lichtenfels called for Paracelsus. From his bed of pain the canon promised a large fee if the Swiss doctor could save his life. Paracelsus threw out all the remedies previously employed and recommended a simple treatment that produced immediate results. The canon recovered his full vigor, and his new strength gave him the courage to refuse payment of the promised fee. Paracelsus promptly took the case to the courts. The judges, influenced by the exasperated physicians, sided with the canon and declared that the remedies used did not justify the bill.

Finding no justice in the court Paracelsus took the opportunity to tell the assemblage exactly what he thought of it. He spoke eloquently in Low German, borrowing the idiom of the market place and the local taproom to emphasize his points. Never was the justification greater nor the remarks more pertinent. The university, the professors, the doctors, the judges, the apothecaries, and human nature in general, were revealed in all their sordidness; nothing was left unsaid.

After this episode the friends of Paracelsus strongly rec-omended that he depart from Basel. The authorities had at last found a tangible charge against him—contempt of court—and they intended to press the advantage. It was either a dungeon or a change of air, so Paracelsus shook the dust of Basel from his shoes and resumed his life of wander-ing. He left town so hastily that he had no time to pack his scientific apparatus.

The next twelve years of his life were spent in almost constant travel. Most of the time he was in dire want. In 1530 he was at Nuremberg, where he came into almost im-mediate conflict with the doctors. He was denounced as an impostor, but discomfited his opponents by curing in a few days some desperate cases of elephantiasis. The records of these cures may still be seen in the city archives of Nurem-berg.

Wherever Paracelsus went his reputation suffered from scholastic criticism and at the same time gained in public esteem. In 1541 he was invited to Salzburg by the lord palatine Ernst, Duke of Bavaria, who was a great lover of alchemy and other secret arts. It seemed that at last the wan-dering physician had found a haven. The duke was intrigued and pleased with his personality. The numerous defects of temperament were generously overlooked, but it seems that fate had not willed that Paracelsus should ever known physical happiness or security. He died after a few months in his new home on the 24th of September, 1541.

The manner in which this remarkable man came to his death is shrouded in mystery. His enemies spread the rumor that he died in a common alehouse as the result of a drunken debauch lasting several days. Most contemporary writers more friendly in their attitudes say that he was thrown down a steep incline by assassins in the pay of physicians and apothe-caries. He was buried in the churchyard of St. Sebastian. Later his remains were removed to a more prominent part of the churchyard and a marble monument was erected to his memory. His grave became a shrine for those seeking remedies for their physical afflictions. On one occasion prayers spoken at his grave are said to have preserved the community from the plague.

Paracelsus was, beyond question, the greatest physician of his day and one of the most original thinkers in the history of medicine. He was a one-man revolution in the world of science, abundantly endowed by nature with the tempera-mental qualities necessary for such an undertaking. Howard Wilcox Haggard, professor of physiology at Yale, writing of the century of great reformers, mentions specifically Luther in religion, Vesalius in anatomy, Pare in surgery, and Para-celsus in therapy.

Paracelsian Philosophy

The philosophy of Paracelsus is a difficult and involved system derived from a variety of sources. By religious con-viction he was a devout Christian, and no question concern-ing his orthodoxy has ever been raised. But in his way of life and in his intellectual convictions he was most certainly a pagan, deriving his principal inspiration from the traditions of Neoplatonism. He is, therefore, an important link in the golden chain of descent by which the modern world is bound to the classical tradition.

His voluminous writings reveal profound scholarship and an intense devotion to essential knowledge. They are not the products of a dabbler or pretender, but are monuments

to careful observation and reflection. It is not known whether
any of these works exist in his own handwriting, as he
dictated nearly everything to his disciple Crollus. In comparison to modern style his essays are interminable, abounding in repetition and loaded with inconsequential detail.
But this was the style of his time, and nearly all medieval
writings are subject to the same criticism. The *Opera* consists of three massive volumes, each exceeding one thousand
pages.

Unfortunately for modern science, only selections from
Paracelsus are available in English. Translators have been discouraged by the magnitude of the undertaking. A few
short tracts appear in early collections of alchemical essays.

It cannot be said that the Paracelsian writings are well-
ordered or related to each other. They are principally fragments recorded from observation or experience. The wandering life of the man was rich in intellectual adventure.
He listened to strange and wonderful accounts about un-
believable things. He investigated these accounts, and if he
found reasonable supporting evidence he recorded them for
the benefit of future times and distant places.

We find what appears to be a general chaos, with alchemy,
magic, cabala, medicine, surgery, astrology, necromancy, and
divination, all jumbled together. Each large and general
statement is supported and amplified by a variety of incidents
and anecdotes. In one place he tells of the skin of a bird
which although nailed to a wall continued to molt its feathers
each year and grow new ones. In another place he describes
a ring made of antimony which, if placed on a sick man's
finger, will absorb the disease and then melt and flow off the
finger like quicksilver.

We learn that grapevines absorb gold from the earth, and this gold can be extracted by burning the vines. He was one of the first to treat syphilis with mercury, and the reader is presented with details of theory and practice. Not far from some sober medical observation is a list of talismans to be fashioned during certain various aspects of the planets. One of these, when worn about the neck, is an infallible remedy for dropsy.

It is all fascinating reading. The style is certainly dogmatic and bombastic, but the scope is encyclopedic. There is no doubt that thousands of useful hints which could be of service today are hidden away in these great folios, laden as they are with daring and original thoughts.

Long and careful study of the Paracelsian corpus reveals a kind of grand system which binds the contradictions together. This larger vision is derived from Neoplatonism. Paracelsus believed the world to be divided into three parts. The first was spiritual, the second sidereal, and the third elementary. In this he followed closely the old Pythagorean viewpoint. Plato shared the same opinion on basic cosmogony. As the world is threefold in its fabric, so all living things are threefold in their constitutions. Man is the noblest of the physical creatures, and he derives his spiritual part from the spirit of the world. His sidereal nature originates among the stars and constellations, and his corporeal body is made up of the four elements. Each of the three worlds is illumined by a sun. The spirit of God, the source of all life and good, is the first of these suns. The universal mind is the second sun, originating among the influences of the planets and stars. The material luminary is the third sun, and is supported by the metaphysical suns which exist invisibly behind and within it.

The world is a macrocosm, a vast being. This being is a god, with a body of light and feet of clay. The material world is merely the visible part of this divine being. Man is a microcosm; a little world patterned after the greater one and corresponding to the universe in all its essential parts. From the hermetic school Paracelsus derived his doctrine of analogies. "As above, so below" was the ancient axiom. By the study of man we discover the mysteries of the universe. By a mystic contemplation of the universe we discover the secret of man. The human being is connected to his spiritual source by the link of intellect, and the use of the mind determines whether the spiritual or the material part of the nature dominates. This is good Socratic reasoning, and one of the most idealistic of all attitudes in regard to man's place in nature.

The spiritual world is not just an empty space filled with the invisible light of God; it is a world populated by creatures abounding in divine qualities. These have been called the archangelic host. To Paracelsus these archangels existed according to race, time, and place. They could be studied and classified, and were a proper subject for intellectual consideration. To strengthen this point he gathered a vast amount of tradition from ancient sources.

Also the sidereal world has its creatures, its races, and its species. To borrow the words of Socrates, these beings lived along the shores of the air as men live along the shores of the sea. The sidereal creatures might involve themselves in human affairs resulting in various phenomena called miraculous. Paracelsus declined to regard miracles as supernatural, but held them to be merely superhuman. His definition was: "A miracle is an effect, the cause of which is unknown, but the cause must be equal in power to the effect which is produced."

Paracelsus was one of the first to study the effect of the imagination on the mental and physical life of the human being. Many of his observations anticipated the findings of modern psychology. The word imagination has the same root as the word magic, and the power of imagery can be developed for the accomplishment of a variety of purposes. He wrote: "Determined imagination is the beginning of all magical operations." The imaginative power is strengthened and sustained by the will. Faith must confirm the imagination and set it in a proper course, for faith establishes the will. In another place he said: "Because men do not perfectly imagine and believe, the result is that the arts are uncertain."

By visualizing inwardly the purpose of life and the goal of human effort man can bring to himself a good or evil destiny according to his use of the imaginative power. The human being images or imagines the form of the world in which he lives. We do not perceive things as they are but as we imagine them to be. Thus if we imagine the world to be evil it becomes evil for us; if we imagine ourselves the victims of injustice this imagining will depress our spirits and cause us to interpret everything that occurs as a personal injustice to ourselves. But Paracelsus went still further; he believed that the imaginations of one person could be transferred to another through the mystery of the astral light. In this way our most secret convictions and beliefs have a power for public woe or weal. This is magic. It is not necessary to draw circles at crossroads or conjure up spirits to do our bidding; the supreme magical art is the control of the imagination by the will of the adept. Paracelsus liked to say, "Magic is a great concealed wisdom, and reason is a great public foolishness."

In his own time Paracelsus was called the Swiss theosophist. Experience revealed to him that a large part of witchcraft and sorcery was really obsession by an idea. A man can be possessed by the demon of his own perverse imagination, yet so great is the power and force of imagery that it can bring about effects in the physical world. Imagination can cause storms, bring about plagues, and corrupt the health of the body. Because the mind is superior to the physical form it has dominion over it and can corrupt it from within. Except such ailments as arise from accident, most sickness is caused by intemperance of the will or through negative or perverted imagination.

It requires only a slight change in terminology to reconcile the viewpoints of Paracelsus with the modern findings of Freud and Adler. The most recent opinions in medicine agree with the Paracelsian doctrine that a great part of sickness arises not in the body but is communicated to it by the intemperances of the intellect.

Magnetic Philosophy

A large part of the philosophy of Paracelsus is devoted to the study of magnetism. The ancients were aware of magnetism principally through the phenomenon of the loadstone. Pythagoras, Plato, and Aristotle, were intrigued by the strange qualities of this stone. According to Pliny the word magnetism or magnet was derived from the name of a shepherd, Magnes. While tending his sheep on Mount Ida, Magnes was amazed when a small stone attached itself to his iron-bound staff. The stone of Hercules, as it was after-

ward called, was said to be under the rulership of the planet
Mars, and a variety of speculations were evolved to explain
its curious properties.

Albertus Magnus believed that Aristotle knew of the
polarity of the magnet, but this has not been substantiated.
There are legends to the effect that ancient mariners navi-
gated their ships by means of iron arrows. Every nation of
importance has laid claim to the invention of the compass.
The case for China is probably the strongest.

The magnetic philosophy of Paracelsus originated in his
speculations about the possible use of magnets in the treatment of disease. Up to his time no one seems to have thought
of the magnet as a means of therapy. He applied magnetized
substances to various parts of the human body according to
certain rules, and claimed to have cured a variety of ailments
in this manner. Having convinced himself of the reality of
magnetic force, he evolved an elaborate philosophy on the
subject. All parts of nature are bound together by a magnetic sympathy. Magnetism is an invisible substance, which
explains how distant bodies may be in sympathy with each
other although not connected in a visible way. Man is bound
to the universe by magnetic sympathy. This is possible because each living thing has within it the polarities of all
other living things. As there are constellations in the sky,
so there are smaller constellations in the human brain, and
these two orders of stars differing in magnitude but identical
in quality are united by the sympathy of similarity. There
is a magnet within each person by which he draws to himself the qualities appropriate to his disposition and nature.
In this way he can draw disease out of space and bind it to
himself.

The quality of the personality magnet is determined by internal consciousness. We draw to us that which is like us. If the will and the imagination be corrupt, the magnetic power of this corruption gathers similar corruption from chaos, and our evils are multiplied.

Diseases have their magnetic qualities; in fact they are entities of magnetism. It is possible to treat disease by transplantation. Magnetism is closely identified with the blood, which Goethe called 'a most peculiar essence'. The Paracelsian technique was to transplant a disease by transferring a part of the infected substance to some neutral media. A few drops of a sick man's blood, if introduced under the bark of a tree, brought no evil to the tree; in fact it might even benefit its growth. Vitalized by the life of the tree the drops of blood became a powerful magnet and could draw to themselves all of the ailment which was afflicting the patient. The result of these speculations was a complete system of sympathetic medicine, which was climaxed a century later by the famous weapon salve of Sir Kenelm Digby. This was a method of treating wounds by applying the medication to the body of the weapon which inflicted the wound, instead of to the body of the victim.

Paracelsus came to regard medicines as carriers of magnetism. It was not the drugs themselves which wrought the cures; rather they set up polarities in the body which drew healthy magnetic forces from the universe to combat the unhealthy magnetic vortexes in the body of the sufferer. He sought to capture the magnetism of the planets in dew which he gathered on glass plates at night when the planets were in certain aspects to each other. This dew was useful only if it did not touch the earth, for such contact demagnetized it and destroyed its subtle virtue.

The magnetic speculations of Paracelsus inspired the system of animal magnetism evolved by Friedrich Anton Mesmer. If we substitute the modern word vibration for the Paracelsian term magnetism, the significance of the Swiss physician's discovery is immediately apparent. He was working with the principles of vibratory sympathy and antipathy, but lacked the terms we use today.

Among the Paracelsians must be included Jan Baptista van Helmont, the discoverer of illuminating gas; Johann Reuchlin, a biblical theosophist who did much to emphasize the mystical content of the Scriptures; Heinrich Cornelius Agrippa, a great magician and cabalist; and Robert Fludd, the English physician and Rosicrucian who extended the research in magnetism. Fludd was one of the men who opposed the materialistic opinions of Johannes Kepler, the astronomer.

A link between Paracelsus and Friedrich Anton Mesmer was Valentine Greatrakes, an Irishman born in 1628. Greatrakes suffered persecution because he was able to cure a variety of diseases by stroking the body with his hands. Robert Boyle, the British physicist and chemist, testified that Greatrakes was able to cure blindness, deafness, paralysis, dropsy, ulcers, and all kinds of fevers, by his knowledge of magnetism.

Johan Gassner, a German Roman Catholic priest, caused much excitement about 1758 by his use of magnetic-spiritual means in curing disease. Hundreds of patients visited him daily. He wore a blue and red flowered cloak and a silk sash. About his neck was a chain containing a fragment of the true cross. On many occasions disease departed from the patient when Herr Gassner politely requested it to leave. In some cases he recommended simple remedies, but for the most part he used nothing more than a knowledge of the direction of the magnetic forces.

Emanuel Swedenborg reveals a definite knowledge of the Paracelsian theories, and Jakob Boehme shows in his writings his constant indebtedness to Paracelsus. The findings of these earlier mystics were gathered into a psychophysical system of therapy by Mesmer. Even Benjamin Franklin investigated the findings of Mesmer in connection with his research in electricity. In recent years hypnotism and suggestive therapy in general have been evolved from Paracelsian hints and suggestions. Modern systems of electric therapy, and those advocating the use of vibration in the treatment of disease, are following in the same path.

No less extraordinary was Paracelsus' opinion about alchemy. He approached the transmutation of metals by a study of the digestive processes in the human body. Man takes into his mouth a variety of food for the nourishment of his body and mind. This food is like the base metals which the alchemist collects for his experiment. Is it any more remarkable that gold can be produced through the union of salt, sulphur, and mercury, than that the corporeal constitution can be preserved by frequent intakings of roast beef and good Flemish wine? A wide variety of food is grist for the human mill, yet man does not resemble that which he eats, nor does the food set up confusion or conflict in his personality. There is only one answer, and that is that the food itself is not the source of nutrition; it is the media for universal energy, and it is this energy which renews life. The digestive processes separate this energy as a neutral force which may then be adapted to the needs of the human system.

Man lives upon life; some parts he sustains by assimilation of food, while other parts are nourished by the light of the sun, the influence of the stars, and the energy in the atmosphere. There are also invisible fountains of nutrition by which the mind and spirit are nourished. In each instance the food must first be digested, that is, the germ extracted from the husk. A neutral vital agent exists in all things and is the life of all things. This agent is the philosophical gold. It is not actually manufactured; it is released through an alchemical process called digestion. This agent is pure magnetism, the vital principle. It might almost appear that Paracelsus was juggling with the theory of vitamins.

Spiritual Alchemy

Besides physical alchemy there is also spiritual transmutation. God is the philosophers' gold. The divine power digested into human nature by faith becomes the life of the soul. Truth digested into the human mind by will and imagination becomes the life of the intellect. In the ultimate the physical, mental, and spiritual life are one essence manifesting differently in the three orders of the world. It is possible to create artificial gold by nurturing or feeding the seed of gold which is present in all bodies.

The German mystic Jakob Boehme made use of the Paracelsian concept in his symbolism of the soul tree. He described the seed of the soul as planted in the human heart. When the light of the spiritual sun touches this seed it germinates and releases its power. The seed grows into a tree when it is nourished by the spiritual and mystical aspirations. All spiritual things grow if they are fed spiritualized vitality.

Paracelsus believed that metals grow in the earth and that the veins of the precious substances spread through the rocks like the branches and twigs of a growing plant. Some years ago I had the privilege of examining a gold plant growing in a sealed retort. It had slowly increased in size until it was about an inch and a half high and resembled in texture a delicate fern. Paracelsus learned from the miners that gold and silver replenish themselves in some strange way, appearing in considerable quantity where a few years before they did not exist. Later alchemists wrote extensively on this theme.

One of the most fantastic of the Paracelsian speculations concerned the creation of an homunculus, an artificial human being which could be fashioned by alchemical means. It would require forty days to generate the homunculus in a glass phial. The creature must be nourished with human blood, and after an appropriate time in its glass womb it could be released to develop like an ordinary child. It is especially noted that the physical education of an homunculus requires extreme care and attention. Of course the story of the homunculus is a philosophical fable. But Paracelsus insisted that all fables which exist according to art and nature are possible as physical operations. According to the accounts given in the early manifestoes of the Rosicrucian order its illustrious founder, the mysterious Father C. R. C., was an homunculus. It is said that he was generated and quickened in a womb of glass.

An ancient formula says, "That which is formed by nature is perfected by art." The homunculus is the philosophical adept; it is the product of the spagyric disciplines. The fable is intended to convey the spiritual end for which the alchemical arts were conceived. The alchemist must nourish the homunculus with his own blood; that is, the soul must be fed by the vital substances of the body.

The Submundanes

Paracelsus gave considerable attention to the submundanes, the creatures which inhabit the four simple elements which make up physical substances. His opinions about these creatures were strongly influenced by his contact with Islamic scholars. He recognized four elements: earth, water, fire, and air. Each of these is a vibratory world of its own, and in each of these worlds species and races of living creatures exist. The submundanes or elementals differ from man in one particular. The human creature is a composite; that is, he has a personality composed of all of the elements ensouled by an immortal spirit. The bodies of the elementals are fashioned from the single element in which they exist. They possess no immortal spirit, but because there is no confusion in their bodies they live to great age and at death are completely reabsorbed into their element.

Paracelsus called the creatures of the earth element gnomes and giants; those of the water element undines and nymphs; those of the fire element salamanders; and those of the air element sylphs. The submundanes are divided into tribes and are ruled over by kings and princes. The gnomes build cities and guard the treasures of the earth. The salamanders, because of their fiery natures, are dangerous to human beings. All of the elementals are capricious, and often play pranks on mortals. They are not essentially evil, although their playfulness is sometimes discomfiting.

He also recognized the existence of artificial elementaries created from the thoughts of men. Most important of these

were the incubus and the succubus. The first was a male and
the second a female entity. Both were evil, and are often
confused with demons. They impel to degenerate action
and are created from the secret evil impulses of mortals.
If we interpret the old accounts of the incubi in terms of
modern psychology we will find that they are equivalent to
complexes and fixations arising from emotional frustrations.

The principal end of alchemical and magical speculation
is the discovery of the philosophers' stone. Paracelsus wrote
of this mystery under the name Azoth, the strange jewel
which he carried in the hilt of his sword. It was in Constantinople that he was initiated into the secret of the Azoth.
The jewel of alchemy is the rose diamond, the stone of great
price. Azoth is in reality the diamond soul of the world.
In man it is the perfected spirit, in nature it is universal
life, and in alchemy it is the universal medicine, the powder
of projection—the Red Lion. Who possesses it possesses the
secret of life, and by its power can transmute all substances
into pure gold. So powerful is the stone that it will transmute one hundred thousand times its own weight.

Paracelsus has been accused of being party to the folly of
the gold makers. But he explains his position by the simple
statement that the philosophers' stone is Christ. As faith
transmutes doubt into perfect belief, as wisdom transmutes
knowledge into truth, and as virtue transforms mortal nature
into an immortal being, so the light of God, the diamond
soul of the world, —if understood and directed by art—raises
all things from a corrupt state to a condition of incorrupti-
bility.

Our principle purpose in this book is to trace the descent
of Platonism and Neoplatonism through the intellectual history of the world. As the veins of gold spread through the

rocks, so the golden tradition has grown and increased throughout the ages. Nourished by the intellectual vitality of devoted scholars the seed of philosophy has grown into a great tree whose fruit is for the healing of the nations.

The mysticism of Neoplatonism permeates all of the writings of Paracelsus, and he applied this spirit particularly to the sciences. He became an interpreter, a 'secretary of nature'. Like the Neoplatonists he was devoted to theurgy, the divine magic. His concept of the universe was in accord with the classical tradition, and like the initiated Greeks he was a pantheistic monotheist. He believed in one God, supreme and all-powerful, manifesting through a secondary order of divinities who were the rulers of the particulars in life and nature. He taught a doctrine of signatures and seals. All physical things bore upon them and within them the stamp and signature of divine power.

To Paracelsus the whole world was like a great book written in a strange language. All the forms in nature were letters and words, and he was really learned who could read this book and discover the one story that was concealed yet magnificently revealed by the words and letters. Foolish scholastics were satisfied to ponder the words of Galen and Avicenna. He challenged the benighted schoolmen to leave the books written by men and turn to the great book written by the finger of God. Why should we suffer and die from opinions in the midst of facts?

Because we have not learned to read the magical alphabet of nature we are inclined to deny its very existence. This is as foolish as to say that the writings of Hippocrates do not exist merely because we have neither the time nor the inclination to study Greek or Latin. Incidentally, Hippocrates was the one authority whose writings met the Paracelsian standard. Hippocrates was an observer; he set up clinics and studied disease at firsthand. He tested his remedies, and he and his sons carefuly recorded the results. This was the type of mind that Paracelsus respected. Hippocrates had learned to read the seals and signatures.

Never were mystical abstractions and physical facts more completely synthesized in one personality than in Paracelsus. He taught magic and at the same time attacked all vagary and superstition. He practiced astrology, and criticized his contemporaries for depending upon unproved theory. He compounded alchemical formulas, and blamed the chemists for their useless prescriptions. All this was because to him the spiritual mysteries were the realities, the solid foundations of all the material sciences. The effects of his doctrines were broad and numerous. All medicine was reformed by the precepts which he laid down.

It is common to borrow from authority that which fits our own prejudices and discard the rest. We admire the politics of Plato and ignore his theology. In the same way we respect Paracelsus for his scientific discoveries and ridicule him for his mystical speculations.

In the eye of the mind we can conjure up a vision of the Swiss Hermes, that pompous little man with his bald head, his bulbous nose, and his awkward, ungainly body. Over his shabby raiment is a short cape much the worse for wear, and a bonnet with a stumpy feather sits jauntily over one ear. He wears the sword of a cavalier and has the manner of a king. "Stupid mortals!" he cries as he swaggers up and down. "Eagerly you eat the husk and throw away the kernel. You grasp at physical knowledge and deny the spiritual foundation of life. You cling to your pills and poultices, and die of physics and emetics. Go ahead and die and see who cares! You will never be wise or happy or healthy until you build a new science upon the wisdom of God. It is God who is the physician, and he has supplied all his creatures with the medicines that are necessary. Depart from the stupid mumbling of traditional science and seek truth along the open road that leads to the greater world."

4

THE ADVANCEMENT OF LEARNING

Francis Bacon

THE quaint little English city of St. Albans stands on the site of Verulamium, the old Roman capital, twenty miles northwest of London. The city was sacked and burned A. D. 61 by the British queen, Boadicea. It was rebuilt in the time of the Roman Emperor Hadrian sometime between 117 and 138, and became a walled city.

In the year 303 a Roman soldier of British birth by the name of Alban was stationed at Verulamium. A British Christian priest, Amphibalus, was being persecuted for the preaching of his faith. Alban was so impressed by the courage and sanctity of this holy man that he became converted to Christianity and helped the priest escape his enemies at the cost of his own life. Alban was brought to the site of the present church and there beheaded. It was from the martyrdom of this Roman soldier that St. Albans received its modern name.

The little church of St. Michael, which was founded in the 10th century, stands within the boundaries of the old Roman city. Its Norman arches rise from old Saxon footings,

FRANCIS BACON

and in an arched niche in the wall of the chancel is a life-size statue of Francis, Baron Verulam, Viscount St. Albans, better known as Lord Bacon.

His lordship is represented in a pensive mood, seated in a great chair. He wears his broad-brimmed hat and wide ruff, and his shoes are ornamented with bows in the form of roses. One morning some years ago when the caretaker opened St. Michael's church he found the statue of Francis Bacon lying on the floor of the chancel. Persons unknown had committed this deed of vandalism. There was an opening in the back of the statue, but the contents, whatever they may have been, had been stolen.

Tourists from all parts of the world visit England and pay homage at the shrines of illustrious men and women, but only a few go to the little church of St. Michael to honor the memory of a man who was one of the noblest births of time. Even fewer ride out from St. Albans along the pleasant country road past the excavations of Roman streets and pavements to the ruins of Gorhambury. In the late afternoon a heavy mist hangs over the countryside; gnarled trees rise from the lush dampness of the rich earth, and shaggy, long-haired sheep graze thereabout. Alone in a meadow stands the present home of the Lords of Verulam. The house with its Grecian columns resembles a county courthouse, and seems strangely out of place. A short distance farther on stand the ancient foundations of Gorhambury. Little remains of the house but one corner, which has the appearance of a squat tower. The original house was of no great size, but there lived old Sir Nicholas Bacon, genial and profound, one of England's wisest statesmen. There Queen Elizabeth brought her court to watch the plays and pantomimes composed for her by young Francis. Later, grown to manhood and power, Francis wrote and rested there. In all England there is no shrine of learning more deserving of remembrance, and none more completely forgotten.

A veil of mystery hangs over the personal history of Francis Bacon, but this is not the appropriate place to enter into an elaborate discussion of the controversy which rages about his origin. It is only fair to the reader, however, to acknowledge that the circumstances of his birth are obscure. A number of Baconians are convinced that he was the son of Queen Elizabeth and Robert Dudley, Earl of Leicester, that his real name was Francis Tudor, and that he was the legitimate heir to the throne of England. These same Baconians have sought to advance his cause as the concealed author of the Shakespearean plays. But Bacon the mystic, the poet, and the chancellor of the Empire of the Muses, belongs outside of our present inquiry. We are concerned with Bacon the Platonic philosopher, the first organized thinker of the English speaking world. For this reason we shall make reference principally to his acknowledged writings and the important commentaries thereon.

Yet it is not possible to estimate a man's works entirely apart from the man himself. We must venture a little way toward an interpretation of Bacon the man if we are to understand Bacon the philosopher.

According to common theory Francis Bacon was born at York House in the Strand, London, on the 22nd day of January, 1561. It is usual to accept the published statement that he was the son of Sir Nicholas Bacon, lord keeper of the great seal and one of the most valued and trusted of the elder statesmen at the court of Elizabeth. His mother, according to this account, was Lady Anne Bacon, the daughter of Sir Anthony Cooke who had been the tutor of Edward VI.

Lady Anne was a woman of unusual education for her time, being especially well-read in the classics.

Although Sir Nicholas was never rewarded by a peerage, he shared the most private confidences of the queen, and as lord keeper exercised an influence beyond his station. Accompanied by her favorite, the Earl of Leicester, and a gay retinue of the court, Elizabeth often rode out to Gorhambury, the modest estate of the lord keeper at St. Albans. On one occasion she appeared unexpectedly with half a hundred attendants. Sir Nicholas murmured apologies to the effect that his establishment had no place for such a number of guests. Elizabeth, who expected the best but seldom supplied the means, remarked petulantly, "My Lord Keeper, your house is not great enough for your person." Sir Nicholas, whose wit was the marvel of his time, bowed solemnly, "Alas, madam, I fear that you have made my person too great for my house."

Elizabeth's visits to Gorhambury were usually under the pretext of state business. It was rather obvious, however, that her principal interest was young Francis, whom she affectionately designated, "My little Lord Keeper."

Even as a small boy Francis possessed the grace and dignity of a courtier. He was slight of body and delicate of constitution, with the eyes of a dreamer and a manner far older than his years. He was a favorite of all the nobles, who had not yet learned to fear his mind.

There is no satisfactory account of Bacon's early schooling, but it is supposed that he learned the humanities from his mother. It is also likely that tutors were appointed for him as appropriate to his estate. He and his half brother Anthony were inseparable, and in later years Anthony was frequently called upon to rescue him from financial difficulties.

Formal education began early in those days, and Francis was only twelve when he and Anthony were entered at Trinity College, Cambridge. The schools of the time were in a lamentable condition of scholastic decadence. The buildings were in foul repair and practically without sanitation. The rooms where the students lived were like cold, clammy cells never touched by the light of the sun. The headmasters were disciplinarians with little understanding of human nature and less interest in the subject. The curriculum was utterly sterile, and most of the rich men's sons led lives of genteel debauchery. The only records preserved by some of these old colleges were accounts of the amount of beer and ale consumed by the student body during a semester.

Francis Bacon endured Cambridge for three years, and during that period developed an intense dislike for the scholastic system. His mind sickened at what passed for learning, and his body sickened because of the unhealthful environment. While he was at Cambridge there was a visitation of the plague, and it was necessary temporarily to close the college. During his Cambridge years he came to his famous conclusion that the beginning of learning was to unlearn that which one had been taught.

At Cambridge he was exposed to liberal doses of Aristotle, but these had little effect upon his mind. He had no real dislike for Aristotle, and refers to the great Greek philosopher with all respect, but he heartily detested the interpretations of Aristotle which dominated the intellectual world. Although Henry VIII had broken the temporal power of the Church of England, the universities were still dominated by the educational policies of the cloister schools. It has been pointed out that although Bacon developed an encyclopedic grasp of near-

ly every branch of knowledge, he was always faulty in his
Aristotle. The Cambridge complex lingered on.

After leaving Trinity College Francis and Anthony entered the society of lawyers at Gray's Inn for the purpose of
establishing themselves in a learned profession. Although
Sir Nicholas held a position of great responsibility the family
was without large means, and it was necessary for the young
men to prepare for independent careers.

When Bacon was about sixteen he was sent abroad with
the British Ambassador to Paris. He remained in France
nearly three years, during which time he gained a practical
insight into the working of European politics. While in
Paris he began his experimentation with state ciphers and
secret methods of writing. At that time he perfected his
celebrated biliteral cipher, which he describes at length in
The Advancement of Learning. Examples of the use of this
cipher are to be found in many of his own books, as well as
in some contemporary publications. It is from the decoding
of his biliteral ciphers that we gain the story of his youthful
infatuation for Margaret, the young princess of Navarre. She
was the one great love of his life, and the hopelessness of this
romance left permanent scars in his personality.

In 1579 Sir Nicholas died suddenly, and Bacon hastened
home to meet the emergencies which resulted. Through
what history regards as an oversight, the lord keeper had not
properly provided for his youngest son. Baconians suggest
that he may have felt that his small estate belonged by right
to his own blood, and that the queen should come forward
and supply her son with appropriate means. But Elizabeth
did nothing, and Francis was little better than penniless.
Poverty has been called the disease of the wise, and throughout his life Bacon was almost constantly in debt. He was

notably imprudent in the handling of money, and the social
requirements of his position demanded a good appearance.
In desperation he borrowed to survive, and had it not been
for the generosity of Anthony his condition would have been
unbearable. Like most intellectuals, young Francis lived in
a world of hopes and ideals. He was not thoughtful in small
matters, but it is not recorded that he ever failed to repay as
rapidly as his finances would permit.

Bacon said of himself, "I thought myself born to be of
advantage to mankind." The first step was to become self-
supporting, so he took apartments with the society of lawyers
at Gray's Inn and entered seriously into the profession of
law. The legal life of 16th-century England was burdened
by the corrupt machinery of the royal court. Justice was at
the mercy of the queen's whims, the queen's favorites, and
the conspiracies in the House of Lords. The formula for
rapid advancement was to select a powerful patron and
flatter one's way through the maze of incompetence and corruption.

Bacon's ultimate success, however, came not from easy
circumstances or strong patronage. He attempted the usual
course but failed miserably, due to his unwise selection of a
patron. According to history Sir William Cecil (Lord Burghley), lord high treasurer of England and one of the most
powerful men in the kingdom, was Bacon's uncle. But he
had a son of his own whom he was seeking to advance.
The younger Burghley was cripplied in one foot and his
physical deformity may have influenced the father in his
behalf. In any event, Bacon's suit developed nothing but
promises and evasions, and the promises were never kept.
Early in his political career he succeeded also in offending the
queen, a most disastrous circumstance. Some say that he was

too outspoken in his political opinions, and the court gossips made sure that Elizabeth received well-colored details. The Baconians suggest that he demanded recognition as Elizabeth's son, and the queen went into a trantrum that lasted for days.

Bacon was forty-four when he proposed marriage to Alice Barnham, whom he described in a letter to Robert Cecil as "An alderman's daughter, a handsome maiden to my liking." Alice, who was not yet twenty, was one of the seven daughters of Lady Packington, an ambitious and cantankerous dowager. After the death of Mr. Barnham of blessed memory, the widow had made a fortunate second marriage, adding Sir Packington's means to the silver plate of her first husband. Lady Packington had already married two of her daughters to titles, and complained bitterly at the thought of her Alice becoming plain Mrs. Bacon. She argued her dissatisfaction with lawyer Bacon, who refused to argue back on the grounds that no qualified attorney would debate without an appropriate fee. Bacon's silence must have proved eloquent, for Lady Packington was finally persuaded, sustained by the thought that her prospective son-in-law stood in line to become the king's attorney. Her ladyship's worst fears were never realized, for in 1603 Bacon was knighted at Whitehall, two days before James VI of Scotland was crowned King of England.

It was not until 1606 that Sir Francis Bacon and Lady Alice Barnham were married in the village church at Martlebone. Bacon's trusted friend and literary associate, Lancelot Andrews, who had been advanced to the bishopric of Chichester, performed the ceremony. Lady Packington was distressed by the absence of certain of the landed gentry, but otherwise the service was a success. Music was supplied by a selected group from Gray's Inn. After the wedding Bacon took his bride to Gorhambury and established her as the mistress of his house. Lady Anne Bacon, then in advancing years, received her daughter-in-law with motherly affection, but was never entirely convinced that the wedding was legal. To the end of her days she insisted that a social scandal was being perpetrated under the family roof.

Some writers have attempted to prove that Bacon's marriage was motivated by ambition to advance his position or estates, but the facts hardly justify such an accusation. The alliance had no political implications, and the Barnhams were country gentry in comfortable circumstances. It would have taxed great wealth to provide a large dowry for seven daughters. We may accept Bacon's own statement that he found in Alice Barnham a maiden to his liking.

There is no indication that Lady Alice Bacon especially influenced the career of her illustrious husband. Little is known of their domestic life. Some writers have assumed that the union was fortunate, and other authorities, equally learned, have insisted that Alice early developed an unruly temper. No children graced the union, and Bacon's own personality so dominated every public circumstance in which he played a part that his domestic fortunes have passed unnoticed.

Bacon's friendship for the impetuous Earl of Essex brought him some advancement and influence, but ended in the tragic trial in which Bacon was forced to prosecute his own friend for high treason. The circumstances of this trial have been used against him, but the truth is that Essex was completely guilty as charged, and Bacon only fulfilled the duties of his office, being sworn to the protection of the crown.

During the long, trying years of struggle Bacon successfully divided his attention between furthering his public career and the development of his philosophical viewpoints. He gained considerable reputation as an author, and drew about himself the best minds of his time. His correspondence was the heaviest of any man in England, and he was in touch with most of the European intellectuals.

Bacon achieved his victory over adversity by the superiority of his intellect alone, and it may be interesting to estimate the extraordinary abilities which he possessed. The fountain of his public power was his skill in language. One writer has said of his literary style that "It is quaint, original, abounding in allusions and witticisms, and rich, even to gorgeousness, with piled-up analogies and metaphors."

Bacon's rare skill in the use of words was recognized by his contemporaries. His friend of many years, Sir Tobias Matthew, penned the following summary: "A man so rare in knowledge, of so many several kinds, endowed with the faculty and facility of expressing it all in so elegant, significant, so abundant, and yet so choice and ravishing a way of words.... perhaps the world hath not seen since it is a world." It is true that even a single sentence extracted from Bacon's writings can with certainty be attributed to him by the purity and originality of the structure.

Bacon's legal writings reveal him to have been a lawyer of outstanding ability. It has been suggested that he was less dogmatic and given to the letter of jurisprudence than some of his contemporaries, but not one of them equaled him in the searching out of justice. He chose to abide by the spirit of legality, and his philosophic mind enabled him to weigh evidence with consummate skill. It was his hope that he would live long enough to digest and codify the whole structure of English law. Although he did not achieve his full purpose he made important contributions which have influenced the legal profession even to our day.

As a literary man Bacon has left a number of short works and a few of greater length which reveal his style to advantage. One of his earliest writings, *Essays or Counsels, Civil and Moral,* he dedicated first to beloved Anthony "That are next myself." This work is regarded as one of the choicest examples of English literature, and the first edition is now rare. All of his writings abound in short, well-turned sayings which have survived as household mottoes. The forms are startlingly reminiscent of the style of the Shakespearean plays, and have given comfort and support to the Baconians.

But it is in philosophy that Bacon excelled all the minds of his time. His legal training fitted him for ordered thinking, and his literary ability enabled him to express his thoughts appropriately and elegantly. Through his philosophy he has exercised his broadest influence on the sciences and arts. Though not primarily a scientist, his opinions and methods have become the principal forces in molding the modern scientific attitude.

After Queen Elizabeth's death in 1603 Bacon's fortunes improved, for in some mysterious way she had thwarted his every purpose. James VI of Scotland, the son of the ill-fated Mary Queen of Scots, was crowned King of England as James I. He was in most respects a total failure as a king. His manners offended the court, he spoke with a broad Scottish burr, and was ridiculed as a porridge eater from the north. He had neither the confidence of his ministers nor the support of his people. Effeminate, timid, and extravagant, he had few of the qualities of a ruler. His one virtue seems to have been that he recognized Francis Bacon's abilities. He advanced Bacon in office eight times, and ennobled him three times.

First the Scottish monarch created Bacon a knight, then elevated him to the peerage in 1618 with the title Baron Verulam, and in 1621 made him Viscount St. Albans. When he was appointed lord high chancellor it placed him in power next to the crown. When the king was away from London Bacon was virtually regent, and for years he exercised an authority almost equal to that of king.

Fate plays strange tricks on mortals. The greatest mind in Europe knelt humbly before one of the feeblest intellects in the land. Never for a moment did Bacon reveal the irony of the situation. He supported James in every possible way, counseling him, pleading for the good of the people, and warning him of the consequences of his follies. In this way Bacon followed in the footsteps of rare old Sir Nicholas. He became the great beacon of the state, always dependable, always respected, but never rewarded in a manner that would free him from economic pressure.

King James saved every available penny for his favorite, the Duke of Buckingham, for whom he had developed an unnatural affection. Buckingham was extravagant, capricious, vain, and fretful. The relationship became not only a court scandal but a public outrage. Heavy taxes were levied upon the already overburdened people to keep Buckingham in fineries. Bacon had to stand by and watch this sorry spectacle. True, the king was devoted to him, but the devotion of James was frequently a liability. Bacon had to carry most of the practical burdens, and stood between an outrageous king and an outraged citizenry.

The chancellor accomplished his difficult task and retained the love of the king and the respect of the populace.

This security was a constant source of envy and concern to the lords, who sensed with growing uneasiness the almost unassailable position which Bacon had attained. The people of England were on the verge of revolt. If revolution came it was possible that he would inherit the government. There is no indication that he ever intended to take advantage of his power. As he always said, "I am the king's man." By nature a scholar, the burdens of the state were already heavy enough.

The famous bribery trial brought to an end Bacon's political career. The circumstances of this unfortunate episode have prejudiced the popular mind against the actual achievements of a truly great human being. As Addison said, "A reader seldom peruses a book with pleasure till he knows whether the writer of it be a black or a fair man." Bacon was convicted upon his own confession set forth in great detail, but the conditions which brought about the confession have not been properly examined. Before we condemn the memory of any person whose life and character have been above reproach, because of one particular offense, it is only fair to examine the matter with all thoroughness.

As the storm gathered, Bacon assumed that the whole plot was a deliberate effort to ruin him. Such schemes were common to his time, and knowing his character to be without blame he was inclined to take the matter lightly. He was certain that he could prove his innocence of guilt before the assembled body of peers. He was in an extremely delicate position, for by his oath of office he was sworn to protect the person and authority of the king. In that capacity he was unable to express his own convictions on many subjects, and was compelled to sign bills that he had voted against in committee.

Corruption was to be expected in high places, and the public mind was accustomed to the burden, but James and his court had abused the royal privileges. The entire government was so undermined by plots and intrigue that the very state was on the verge of collapse. Both the king and the lords knew that a head must fall to restore public confidence, and there were only two heads important enough to satisfy the populace—the king's and the lord high chancellor's. The plan was to throw Bacon to the lions.

Bacon was popular with the people, and the first step was to turn public opinion against him. He was charged with the acceptance of bribes and the corruption of his office. His accusers for the most part were enemies of years' standing. The witnesses against him were either hired perjurers or disgruntled suitors who had lost their cases in chancery. One witness was a convicted forger and extortioner by name Churchill. This man was in such bad odor that even the lords shuddered at his presence.

So flagrant and obvious was the machinery of the plot that Bacon continued in his attitude of humorous contempt. He knew that no reputable witness could be found who would testify that his decisions as lord high chancellor had ever been influenced by gifts or bribes. In fact, after three hundred years and the examination of all of the cases in which Bacon figured, no evidence has been found that he ever compromised a decision for his own advantage. It was customary for all public officials to receive gifts from grateful clients or from those hoping to receive special consideration. Bacon acknowledged this system to be corrupt but inevitable as long as the state did not compensate public officials in a way that would permit them to maintain themselves according to the responsibilities of their stations.

Bacon believed that when the time came he could clear himself absolutely and bring about the final discomfiture of his archenemy, the jealous and vindictive Sir Edward Coke, and his associates. He most certainly would have succeeded had it not been for the king. It was necessary for Bacon to decide between the vindication of his own name and the preservation of his monarch. He was under oath to sustain the dignity and order of the state. For this consideration he sacrificed his own reputation. James on bended knee implored him to save the ruling house of England by pleading guilty to crimes which he had not committed. It was the most difficult decision that Bacon ever made. But after mature deliberation he resolved to sacrifice himself. He framed his complete confession, answering each of the twenty-eight articles of the charge, and although the most brilliant and subtle lawyer in Europe he made no effort in his own defense.

It is interesting to note in reviving Bacon's confession that while he acknowledged the corruption of his office by a general statement, there is no acknowledgment of corruption to any of the twenty-eight particular accusations. The confession is in reality merely the acknowledgment of the acceptance of gifts, in some cases bestowed long after the termination of the case. A careful reading of the confession will make it evident to any fair-minded person that the chancellor most certainly could have defended himself successfully had he been so minded.

Found guilty upon this curious confession, Bacon was fined forty thousand pounds, sentenced to imprisonment in the tower during the king's pleasure, declared incapable of any public office, and deprived of his seat in Parliament. The action of the king gives a clear indication of the facts of the case. James forgave the fine, Bacon's imprisonment in the tower lasted only three days, and though it is not generally known Bacon did sit again in the House of Lords on at least one occasion. The office of lord high chancellor was abolished, and no man took Bacon's place. It was not the penalty, but the conviction that was sought. This attained, the rest was forgiven.

It is difficult to keep the secrets of a royal court from the knowledge of the people. Bacon left London quietly, and was received at St. Albans not as a disgraced man but as a public hero. He lost none of his friends and very little of his influence. In fact, his conviction released him from the thankless burdens of a political career. Settled quietly at Gorhambury, he resumed the real work of his life. As philosopher and scholar he continued his imperishable contributions to the intellectual and cultural progress of his world. He continued to enjoy the friendship of his king, and in a letter to him James wrote that his value to England was infinitely greater as a scholar than it ever could be as a politician.

According to history, Bacon lived five years after the termination of his public office. Always frail of health, the burdens of state had drained his physical resources. Although continually harassed by lack of funds, he continued his literary activities with some small assistance from the king, and a number of his finest writings belong to this period.

In the spring of 1626 Bacon went to London, and while there the thought came to his mind that snow might be useful for the preserving of meat. To further his experiments he purchased a dressed fowl from a villager and stuffed it with snow. In handling the snow he contracted a severe cold.

The chill brought on bronchitis from which he died a few days later, April 9, 1626.

A careful reading of contemporary reports indicates that there was considerable uncertainty concerning Bacon's death. At least three accounts exist, differing even as to the place of his death. There is no satisfactory account to his funeral, although most of the outstanding men of his day penned extravagant tributes to his genius. These tributes frequently refer to him as the greatest poet of his time, although only a half dozen short and unimportant verses have been with certainty attributed to him.

There is a strong tradition held by a number of Baconians that Bacon did not die in England, but choosing to be considered dead moved to Holland where he lived under an assumed name for at least ten years, devoted to the activities of a secret society which he had founded.

High Chancellor of Nature's Laws

It has been said that the English language first became a vehicle of philosophical literature by the publication of Bacon's *Advancement of Learning* in 1605. It cannot be shown, however, that he did a great deal to popularize national languages as a means to disseminate culture. Most of his important writings were published first in Latin, which he preferred as the tongue of scholarship.

The 17th century was an era of new foundations in thinking. Throughout Europe isolated intellectuals were developing along the lines of humanistic philosophy. At this point mention should be made of the French philosopher René Descartes (1596-1650). Bacon and Descartes are often referred to as sharing honors in the establishment of the scientific viewpoint, but in the Cartesian system (the philosophy of Descartes) much greater emphasis was laid on the nature of God as the source of all certainty in the mind. Descartes advanced one interesting and peculiar observation; he used spelling as an example of the mental process. A man writing along thoughtless of spelling is likely to spell correctly, but if he hesitates and ponders the construction of a word he will pass into a state of uncertainty. The more he thinks and isolates the single word in his mind the greater will be his confusion, and misspelling will almost certainly result.

We are surrounded at all times by what appear to be orders of fact. These remain certainties until we isolate them and think each one through. Immediately uncertainties are generated, resulting in an aphorism to the effect that the more we think the less we know. For this reason the ignorant live in a world of uncertain certainties which they never question, but the wise inhabit a sphere of certain uncertainties which are a constant annoyance to the intellect. Descartes set up a method for the definition of the boundaries of fact by which the mind might have a number of basic truths on which to build the superstructure of a broad learning. His opinions contributed considerably to the philosophy of Immanuel Kant, and in this way the stream of the Platonic descent was enriched.

Although Descartes was in certain respects influenced by scholasticism, Bacon was comparatively free of this older system of philosophy. Formal scholasticism had entered its last phase and was breaking down in all its branches and departments. Henry VIII had helped to clear the way for Bacon in England by breaking the power of the Church to dominate the intellectual life of man. The mind, free of the arbitrary limitations of theology, was exploring a variety of doctrines. Bacon did not claim to be an original thinker, nor to have originated the basic theories which he promulgated. He defined himself and his position by saying that he rang the bell that brought the wits together.

An engraving of Bacon by Watts appears in a number of early editions of Bacon's writings. The portrait shows him seated at a table wearing his familiar hat. Above his head is a wreath bearing the inscription, *The Third Great Mind Since Plato*. There is no indication as to the identity of the second mind; possibly Aristotle is intended.

The New Instrument of Knowledge

In the *Novum Organum* (the new instrumentality for the acquisition of knowledge) Bacon classified the intellectual fallacies of his time under four headings which he called *Idols*. He distinguished them as *Idols of the Tribe, Idols of the Cave, Idols of the Marketplace,* and *Idols of the Theater.* An idol is an image, in this case held in the mind, which receives veneration but is without substance in itself. Bacon did not regard idols as symbols, but rather as fixations. In this respect he anticipated modern psychology.

Idols of the Tribe are deceptive beliefs inherent in the mind of man, and therefore belonging to the whole of the human race. They are abstractions in error arising from common tendencies to exaggeration, distortion, and disproportion. Thus men gazing at the stars perceive the order of the world, but are not content merely to contemplate or record that which is seen. They extend their opinions, investing the starry heavens with innumerable imaginary qualities. In a short time these imaginings gain dignity and are mingled with the facts until the compounds become inseparable. This may explain Bacon's epitaph which is said to be a summary of his whole method. It reads, "Let all compounds be dissolved."

Idols of the Cave are those which arise within the mind of the individual. This mind is symbolically a cavern. The thoughts of the individual roam about in this dark cave and are variously modified by temperament, education, habit, environment, and accident. Thus an individual who dedicates his mind to some particular branch of learning becomes possessed by his own peculiar interest, and interprets all other learning according to the colors of his own devotion. The chemist sees chemistry in all things, and the courtier ever present at the rituals of the court unduly emphasizes the significance of kings and princes.

The title page of Bacon's *New Atlantis* (London 1626) is ornamented with a curious design or printer's device. The winged figure of Father Time is shown lifting a female figure from a dark cave. This represents truth resurrected from the cavern of the intellect.

Idols of the Marketplace are errors arising from the false significance bestowed upon words, and in this classification Bacon anticipated the modern science of semantics. According to him it is the popular belief that men form their thoughts into words in order to communicate their opinions to others, but often words arise as substitutes for thoughts and men think they have won an argument because they have outtalked their opponents. The constant impact of words variously used without attention to their true meaning may in turn condition the understanding and breed fallacies. Words often betray their own purpose, obscuring the very thoughts they are designed to express.

Idols of the Theater are those which are due to sophistry and false learning. These idols are built up in the field of theology, philosophy, and science, and because they are defended by learned groups are accepted without question by the masses. When false philosophies have been cultivated and have attained a wide sphere of dominion in the world of the intellect they are no longer questioned. False superstructures are raised on false foundations, and in the end systems barren of merit parade their grandeur on the stage of the world.

Baconians are inclined to believe that Bacon's allusions to the theater refer to his participation in the Shakespearean plays. This is not necessarily true, as a careful reading of the *Novum Organum* will show. Bacon used the theater with its curtain and its properties as a symbol of the world stage. It might even be profitable to examine the Shakespearean plays with this viewpoint in mind.

After summarizing the faults which distinguish the learning of his time, Bacon offered his solution. To him true knowledge was the knowledge of causes. He defined physics as the science of variable causes, and metaphysics as the science of fixed causes. By this definition alone his position in the Platonic descent is clearly revealed. Had he chosen Aristotle as his mentor the definition would have been reversed.

It was Bacon's intention to gather into one monumental work his program for the renewal of the sciences. This he called *Instauratio Magna* (the encyclopedia of all knowledge), but unfortunately the project was never completed. He left enough, however, so that other men could perfect the work.

The philosophy of Francis Bacon reflects not only the genius of his own mind but the experiences which result from full and distinguished living. The very diversity of his achievements contributed to the unity of his thinking. He realized the importance of a balanced viewpoint, and he built his patterns by combining the idealism of Plato with the practical method of Aristotle. From Plato he derived a breadth of vision, and from Aristotle a depth of penetration. Like Socrates, he was an exponent of utility, and like Diogenes a sworn enemy of sophistry. Knowledge was not to be acquired merely for its own sake, which is learning, but for its use, which is intelligence. The principal end of philosophy is to improve the state of man; the merit of all learning is to be determined by its measure of usefulness.

Bacon believed that the first step was to make a comprehensive survey of that which is known, as distinguished from that which is believed. This attitude he seems to have borrowed from Paracelsus and shared with Descartes. Knowledge may be gathered from the past through tradition. It may be accumulated and augmented by observation, but it must be proved and established by experimentation. No theory is important until it has been proved by method. Thus Bacon set up the machinery of control which has since become almost the fetish of science.

Upon the solid foundation of the known, trained minds can build toward universal knowing, which is the end of the work. Knowledge alone can preserve and perfect human life. In spite of his scientific approach, Bacon in no way discounted the spiritual content in the world. Knowledge might arise from inspiration and the internal illumination of the consciousness, but this illumination is not knowledge until, through experimentation, the truth is physically established.

Bacon's Mystical Convictions

In his essay on atheism Bacon wrote: "I had rather believe all the fables in the *Legend,* and the *Talmud,* and the *Alcoran,* than that this universal frame is without a mind. And therefore God never wrought miracles to convince atheism, because his ordinary works convince it. It is true that a little philosophy inclineth man's mind to atheism, but depth in philosophy bringeth man's mind about to religion. For while the mind of man looketh upon second causes scattered, it may sometimes rest in them and go no further. But when it beholdeth the chain of them, confederated and linked together, it must needs fly to providence and Deity."

William Rawley, D. D., for many years Bacon's chaplain and personal friend, appends his *Life of Bacon* to his edition of Bacon's *Resuscitatio.* This biography includes many intimate details about Bacon's mind and method of writing. Rawley's tribute to the mysticism of his master is worth remembering in this day when scientists boast of their materialism. "I have been enduced to think," writes the good chaplain, "that if there were a beam of knowledge, derived from God, upon any man in these modern times, it was upon him. For though he was a great reader of books, yet he had not his knowledge from books, but from some grounds and notions from within himself. Which, notwithstanding, he vented with great caution and circumspection."

In his writings Bacon labored with great care, striving for perfection of knowledge rather than of style. Yet in the end he achieved both. In preparing the outline for the *Instauratio* he prepared twelve copies, revising the material year by year before he committed it to the press. He kept extensive notebooks in which he recorded observations and experiments, and brief statements of his own, together with quotations from other authors. He seldom read for any great length of time, but discovering in some author a passage which pleased him he would leave his desk and walk in his garden or be driven through the countryside in his coach. These interludes were his principal form of recreation.

There can be little doubt that Bacon made practical use of Paracelsus and his doctrine of practical experience. There is considerable similarity in the writings of the two men; each gathered up a diversity of fragments relating to almost every possible subject, and distilled from these collections the elements of their philosophy. Bacon believed that the complexity of the physical universe was in appearance rather than in fact. Basic forms are limited in number and are a kind of alphabet. By the combinations of forms, words are produced in an infinite diversity, and from these words the whole language of nature is manifested. The important task is to discover with certainty the basic letters and the rules governing their combinations.

Bacon uses the word "form" in an unusual way. Even his own definitions are not entirely clear. A form is a definite pattern, basic in nature and not susceptible to further reduction. The compounding of forms obscure their original natures, and the human senses beholding the compounds are lured into error.

To my mind one of the most important of Bacon's aphorisms is, "Nature is subdued only by submission." In other words, man masters the world by obeying the laws governing the world. This is a simple Platonic statement and lies at the root of all great systems of idealistic philosophy. Bacon extends the thought by reminding the reader that perfect obedience or submission is impossible without knowledge of the laws to be obeyed. The purpose of science is to render scientific the process of obedience.

Science is the Image of Truth

Science is nothing more than the image of truth. Absolute truth is truth of being, and relative truth is truth of knowing. These differ only as a direct ray of light differs from a refracted ray; thus the difference is in degree rather than in substance. Science corresponds to the refracted ray because it is truth which has passed through nature and man.

Bacon advocated experience and Descartes advocated speculation as the means of discovering truth. Both methods have survived, but speculation is now limited to those fields which lie beyond the possibility of present experience. Scholastic philosophy was almost entirely speculative and wandered afield because it failed to set up the proper machinery to estimate experience.

Nature presents itself to the human understanding as a direct ray of light. We see about us at all times certain facts, in themselves useful but not in themselves complete. To accept nature as all is an error. To refuse nature and take refuge in abstract theology is equally wrong. It is not given to man to perceive God directly, but the divine will is reflected from the face of nature and may be examined indirectly. Thus it appears that Bacon did not break with religion; in fact, he bestowed a dignity upon religious fact far greater and more reasonable than theology ever imagined.

In his search for essentials Bacon accumulated a variety of interesting lore. In *The History of Life and Death* he examined ancient and modern examples of longevity in an effort to determine the form of human submission which extended the duration of life. In the *Natural History of Winds* he explored the phenomena of atmosphere. And in the *Sylva Sylvarum* he gathers a quantity of notes relating to natural history. His purpose in each instance was to discover the form behind the phenomena—the pattern governing the complex.

While it is not possible for the average person to follow all of Bacon's processes, there are certain conclusions concerning the morality of thinking which are practical for all. He advised each human being to live thoughtfully and to search for the universal realities that lie concealed within and beneath the commonplace. By observation and thought life can become meaningful, and each can preserve himself from common faults and contribute to the security and improvement of others.

It is more important to think one small thought through to its reasonable end than to accept without examination a brilliant solution submitted by another. We grow by thinking, not by agreeing or by accepting. The thoughts of others may be important, but they are not valuable to us until we have justified them by personal application. That which is beyond application is unprofitable.

It is important also to divide clearly in our minds that which is known by experience and that which is accumulated from hearsay. Before accepting as true any report on any subject we should ask ourselves, "Do I know this to be true by experience?" Information which cannot be maintained by this criterion need not be rejected, but should be held separate from fact lest we become worshipers of idols.

In our day facts are more available than in the time of Bacon, but conversely, they are subject to many more distortions. We are more swayed by public and private opinion than ever before. It is good to be attentive to all opinions, but a disaster to attempt to live according to their conflict. To be swayed by the motion of the masses is to lose our own center and become the victim of our times.

Bacon, the Neoplatonist

The place of Francis Bacon in the Platonic and Neoplatonic descent is rather obvious. He restated the Platonic doctrine of ideas—that all particulars are suspended from generals in nature. But he simplified these generals, bringing them within the province of the mind. He called men to the discovery of their own estate in nature. He did not regard philosophy as an endless quest, to be perfected only in eternity. He believed perfection to be imminent and attainable. A complete system of thinking is possible now, although new applications of it may develop throughout time. Once the mind is on the right track, doubts end and certainties appear. Upon these certainties men can build indefinitely without need for periodic renovation of their beliefs. Discord in knowledge will end, and energy may be conserved for the essential task and not dissipated in pointless controversy.

When man desires truth as wholeheartedly as he now defends his false opinions, truth will be available. Truth is not distant, but present in all things awaiting discovery. The simplest way to discover truth is to be receptive rather than belligerent in the quest. The universe will not be taken by storm, but will reward obedience with the richest of her treasures.

Although the published writings of Francis Bacon are not especially concerned with theology or metaphysics, his influence in these spheres was considerable. By drawing a clear line of demarcation between reason and faith, he clarified questions which had confused the minds of men for thousands of years. It is useless to direct the reasoning power toward that which is beyond its province. Ultimates must be experienced by faith alone. The trained mind can avoid certain errors common to untrained belief, but it cannot explore the world of spiritual abstraction. Faith must stand as man's link with the infinite. It is at the root of reason, preserving the reasonableness of nature and justifying the struggle of the intellect to know.

In metaphysics Bacon's writings have been a constant fountain of inspiration and idealism. The heroic stature of his mind has attracted the admiration of most idealists. His method has given form and pattern to metaphysical speculation, bringing it within the boundaries of universal law and order. Emphasis upon utility, which is present throughout his writings, has helped to release mysticism from its bondage to abstraction. The average mystic is more concerned with his own internal experiences than the furtherance of human society. He enriches his inner life, but is content with this enrichment and seldom translates his faith into action. Bacon's influence has accomplished much in breaking down metaphysical isolationism.

It has been said that the effect of Bacon's teachings was both immediate and lasting. He is referred to, quoted, and certain of his ideas borrowed, by most of the scientists and philosophers who have followed him in time. The immediate effect of his method is thus evident. In his last will and testament he bequeathes himself to posterity, "For my name and memory I leave it to men's charitable speeches, and to foreign nations, and the next ages."

Dr. Rawley said of Sir Francis Bacon, "To give the true value to his lordship's worth, there were more need of another Homer." This is the estimation of those who knew him well, shared his thoughts, and labored with him for the common good. If his philosophy can be summarized in a single statement it may be found in his own words from the *Novum Organum,* "Knowledge and human power are synonymous, since the ignorance of the cause frustrates the effect."

It is rare to find a man who can attain greatness in several departments of learning. In the case of Bacon we find combined in equal excellence the orator and the writer, the philosopher and the scientist, the statesman and the poet. These diverse interests would doubtless have destroyed a lesser mind, but Bacon ordered his life with his own philosophy. Prudent in success, patient in adversity, he combined the breadth and depth of his thinking with the simple model of a gentle Christian spirit.

It is not known that Bacon ever spoke critically or unkindly of any man. On one occasion King James asked his opinion of the character of a certain statesman recently deceased. This man had been Bacon's enemy and a doubtful servant of the state. Bacon replied that he feared the deceased would never have made His Majesty's estate any better, but would certainly have tried to keep it from being worse. This is probably Bacon's harshest criticism. Nor did he work for the ruin of any other person, nor attempt to advance his own interest at the expense of another. It is interesting, especially in the light of the charges against him, that although many of his legal decisions were appealed, not one was ever reversed.

Diversity Within Unity

In our age of specialization it is deemed inadvisable for a man to divide his interests; success demands single-pointed effort. Yet Bacon is the proof that diversity of interests is not only possible but important to the balance of the mind. This diversity, however, must be enclosed within a unity of purpose. Where vision is lacking confusion is inevitable. But philosophy binds all knowledge to the common purpose of utility.

Bacon will always belong to the next ages. He was the first great Brahman of the West, and two hundred years later another was to arise worthy of sharing this title—Ralph Waldo Emerson.

Bacon as one of the great leaders of human thought can never be separated from his philosophy. He was a part of it. It was his own personal power, as much as his ideas, that changed the mind of his time. He stands before the world, his robes of state damasked with the roses of the Tudors. Long curling hair frames the brow of a sage and falls in ringlets on his wide white ruff. In one hand he carries the seal of Great Britain in a tasseled pouch, and in the other a slender gold-topped cane. With gentle humility he bows before the English throne, "The only gift which I can give Your Majesty is that which God hath given to me; which is a mind, in all humbleness, to wait upon your commandments."

Several modern writers with a flair for psychology have attempted to explain Bacon's extraordinary career by suggesting that he suffered from the consequences of a dual personality. These scribes would convince us that he was, in truth, two men in one body. The first, the noblest and most learned of his age; the second a scheming, self-seeking politician finally caught in the net of his own misdeeds.

Conflicting historical accounts are thus advanced to prove a conflict in the man himself. But the more deeply we study Bacon's life and works, the more apparent it becomes that he was a completely unified human being. Although he excelled in several departments of knowledge, his numerous roles were suspended from one sovereign purpose. Necessity often dictated his selection of methods, but the ends to be accomplished were clear and unchanging. He played many parts, always with consummate skill, and this very skill has influenced adversely the minds of most historians. His purposes were all parts of one purpose—the restoration of the philosophic empire.

JAKOB BOEHME

5

THE MYSTICAL TRADITION

THE word mysticism is derived from the Greek *mystes* which means to shut the eyes, and in a more general sense was applied anciently to the philosophy of those who had been initiated into the mysteries. The mysteries were rituals, pageants, and theatrical performances, designed to enlighten the consciousness through the beholding of divine matters.

Mystical theories are difficult of explanation because they refer to a feeling or thought which is beyond the normal experience of man. There are two kinds of mysticism, the first philosophic and the second religious. Philosophic mysticism is speculative, and is devoted to the problem of man's participation in the consciousness of God. Religious mysticism is termed practical because it is a way of life based upon a complete passive submission to the will of Deity.

The Orient is the natural home of mystical tradition. Both Brahmanism and Buddhism alike taught the unreality of material life and material ambition. The supreme accomplishment was the absorption of the personal self into the consciousness of universal being. The Taoism of China is

131

grounded in the same basic conviction, though in practice it has taken on a magical intellectualism. The Persian Sufis and the Dervishes of Arabia are the most important of the Near-Eastern mystics. With them art, music, and literature modify the severity of the mystical tradition, and they have been considerably involved in speculative idealism.

The Greeks were not by nature mystics. They loved nature and found physical living a happy and satisfactory state. Mysticism flourishes in an atmosphere of frustration, and the classical Greeks had few inhibitions. Possibly Pythagoras came the nearest to the mystical viewpoint, but he was too much of a scientist and philosopher to be completely dominated by divine enthusiasm. If the theological writings of Plato had been more generally read and understood he would have been included among the practical mystics. As it is, he is remembered chiefly as an idealist struggling with the problem of perfecting a system of philosophical government.

The opening centuries of the Christian era brought with them a general collapse of classical culture. To the degree that the difficulties of physical living increased, the natural mysticism in human consciousness was strengthened. The North African city of Alexandria became the center of the intellectual world. Scholars came from all of the Mediterranean countries to study in the great libraries which had been established there under the patronage of the Pharaohs. Greek masters set up their schools, and a golden era of learning resulted. But Alexandrian scholarship was shadowed by an all-pervading melancholy. The era of happy pantheism was coming to an end. The anguished voice of the oracle cried out, "Great Pan is dead."

The Alexandrian intellectuals were fighting for a lost cause. They realized this, and by this very realization they were turned from the enjoyments of physical life and took refuge in the mystical tradition. Neoplatonism came into existence through the mingling of Plato's idealistic philosophy and the mystical speculations of Asia. The rite of primitive Christianity with its emphasis upon sin, death, and suffering, and its doctrine of salvation by grace alone, set the mind in a frustration that was to dominate the world for more than a thousand years.

It remained for Francis Bacon to offer a workable solution for the reconciliation of philosophy and mysticism. By setting up faith and reason in their proper relationship to each other he cleared the way for a balanced pattern of living. Consciousness can extend beyond the limits of the reason to discover as fact that which the intellect cannot grasp as thought. The mystical experience is everywhere present in the life of man and nature. Thought may rise from inspiration or it may end with inspiration.

There is a mystical factor nearly always present in the compound of greatness. This is especially true of the arts, where technique fails unless apprenticed to creative genius. The very origin of reason is a mystery, but we have trained ourselves to ignore the origin of our impulses. Bacon referred to the spiritual powers at the root of life as 'fixed causes', and infers that they may be discovered by faith alone. The universe was not created by intellect, but by a spirit behind intellect. It is this spirit which the mystic seeks in meditation.

Neoplatonism taught an exalted kind of mysticism by which the mind first perfected in reason, then sought to explore the 'Father Fountains' from which the reason flowed. These fountains were the gods; not persons, but beings; not intellects, but spirits in spirit.

The danger of mysticism is that it may arise in a personality unequipped to maintain its force. This leads to a variety of difficulties. The mystic may not be able to interpret in thought or in words the experiences of his inner life. For this reason the Neoplatonists insisted that the mystical vision should not be cultivated until the intellect had been strengthened to meet the pressure of the God-power from within.

Mysticism is not a creed. It is an experience which may occur to the followers of any faith. All religions are susceptible of mystical interpretation, and each has produced a few outstanding mystics. A theology has no spiritual force until its doctrines have been enlightened by the power of God in the heart of the believer.

Most outstanding mystics have been comparatively unlearned in the religions, philosophies, and sciences dominant in their time. If the mind be obsessed by the importance of materially acquired knowledge, it lacks the profound humility which lies at the source of mysticism. The power of the mystical way of life lies in its very simplicity, its gentleness, and the deeply reverent spirit which it produces. These pious and humble impulses are not natural to schoolmen devoted to a competition of ideas. And the passiveness which comes with illumination is interpreted as weakness by those who have not experienced its strength.

The mystical experience cannot be conveyed from one person to another, nor can mysticism be learned from books, yet something of its power can be discovered by a consideration of the gentle lives of the mystics themselves. Let us, therefore, contemplate as a mystery, a ritual in the spirit, the life and work of Jakob Boehme of ancient Gorlitz, the greatest mystic since Jesus Christ.

The Flash of Divine Lightning

In the opening years of the 17th century the small Prussian city of Gorlitz was a struggling community with narrow cobblestone streets and tall, gaunt houses that leaned wearily against each other. Storks built their nests among the chimney pots, and hogs gathered in the principal square to select their menu from the local garbage. Over this municipality ruled the rotund burgomaster with the golden chain of his office. He regarded himself equal in importance to the lord elector, and preferred to be addressed as Worshipful and Truly Sapient.

The city council (which refered to itself as The Noble Right Worshipful Respectable Highly and Much Celebrated and Very Gracious Gentlemen of the Senatorial Administration) served with the burgomaster. This exalted body of stolid burghers was made up of local merchants and artisans with long brown coats and square-toed shoes.

The municipal government was under the thumb of Gregorius Richter, who enjoyed the title Pastor Primarius of Gorlitz. So uncertain was this reverent gentleman's temper and disposition, and so fervent his piety, that the eternal salvation of the entire community was constantly threatened. The local Lutheran clergy included several other reverent masters, one of whom was Alias Dietrich. He was a God-fearing man, but his greater terror was reserved for Parson Richter.

Also worthy of mention is Dr. Tobias Koeber, a most conscientious physician, who bestowed the fullness of his art upon all of the sick regardless of their financial estate. When things got out of hand Dr. Koeber would send to Zittau and call in Dr. Melchior Berndt for consultation. What these two men could not accomplish was left in the hands of God.

It was in this smug provincial orthodox Lutheran community, burdened with all the intolerance that the times were heir to, that the flash of divine lightning struck. It would not seem that a less propitious environment could have been selected. Here Jakob Boehme, the Teutonic theosopher, lived and worked, suffered and died. This was the mortal frame of his immortal vision. Loved and admired, feared an despised, a humble cobbler walked with God in the little town of Gorlitz.

Jakob Boehme was born in the market town of Alt-Seidenberg in Upper Lusatia about nine miles from Gorlitz, in the year 1575. His father's name was Jakob and his mother's name was Ursula. Both were peasants of impoverished circumstances, but a great point has been made of their being good Christian folk, legally married. Little Jakob was brought up in the strict Lutheran faith, and his parents taught him enough of reading and writing so that he could study the Scriptures. It is said that he had some elementary schooling, but the details are not recorded. Education played very little part in the community life except with regard to the clergy.

As soon as he reached sufficient size he was assigned to the task of herding cattle. He would take the herds out into the green fields and hills and sit quietly with them all through the long days. Sometimes other lads from the village accompanied him, but he liked to wander off and commune with himself. One day a curious circumstance occurred. It was about noon and he had climbed a hill which was called Land's Crown. Suddenly he spied a doorway into the earth. The aperture was lined with large red stones overgrown with bushes. Entering the cave he saw a large wooden platter filled to overflowing with golden coins. Fearing that this money belonged to some demon or evil spirit trying to tempt him into sin, he hastened from the place without touching the money. Later a general search was made for the cavern, but it could not be found. Boehme told one of his friends that years afterward a foreign treasure hunter discovered the gold, but the money had been cursed and the foreigner met a terrible death.

It has been suggested that Boehme's experience with the platter of gold was his first adventure into the mystery of the astral light. Perhaps it was a prophetic symbol of his life's work. He was to search the depth of the Holy Scriptures for the lost treasure of the Christian spirit.

Jakob's father, observing that his son was a thoughtful and serious-minded boy, did everything possible to develop and unfold his mind. In addition to a little schooling there were daily prayers at the table, regular church attendance, and weekly discussions of the Bible. When he was about fourteen it was necessary for the family to make some decision about his future. Jakob, though not sickly, did not have a robust constitution. His body was short and heavy, his forehead rather low, his face full, and his nose slightly crooked. It was his eyes that gave promise of the future; they were pale gray, deep-set, and calm as placid pools.

Obviously the boy had not the strength of physique to be a successful farmer, so he was apprenticed to be a shoemaker. Alt-Seidenberg specialized in the making of shoes, and the cobblers had class preference over the farmers. This fortunate apprenticeship was a step upward on the ladder of society. Jakob served his master well, learned his trade quickly and thoroughly. It was simple but sufficient work, and the young

man could think of many strange and distant things while
sitting at his bench pegging boots.

One afternoon he was alone in the little shop when a
stranger, poorly dressed but otherwise respectable, came in to
buy a pair of shoes. The stranger selected footgear to his
liking, and asked the price. But the apprentice was afraid to
fix a value without the permission of his master. The pur-
chaser insisted, however, and at last Jakob named a sum
which he felt certain was more than sufficient. His purpose
was to delay the sale, but the stranger paid the money immediately, and taking the shoes left the shop.

After walking a few steps the unknown man stopped
short, and turning about called out in a deep and serious
voice, "Jakob, come out hither to me." The boy, startled
that his name should be known to the stranger, went out to
the street. The man looked long into Jakob's face, and then
taking him by the right hand said solemnly, "Jakob, thou
art little, but thou shalt become great, and a man so very
different from the common cast that thou shalt be the wonder
of the world. Be therefore a good lad; fear God, and rever-
ence his word. Let it especially be thy delight to read the
Holy Scriptures wherein thou art furnished with comfort and
instruction, for thou shalt be obliged to suffer a great deal of
affliction, poverty, and persecution also. Nevertheless, be
thou of good comfort, and firmly persevere, for God loveth
thee, and he is gracious unto thee."

This was the second of the strange happenings that were
to influence the destiny of Jakob Boehme. The identity of
the mysterious stranger has never been discovered. Likely
enough he was one of those wandering mystics, adepts in
esoteric lore, of which there were many in Europe. Several
old writers mention them—cabalists, magicians, and alchem-

ists, who appeared seemingly from nowhere and vanished again after imparting some choice fragments of wisdom.

Boehme was twenty-five when the third extraordinary experience occurred in his life. One day in his house he chanced to look up toward a pewter dish on a wall rack. The sunlight struck the dish and its dazzling reflection affected his eyes in a remarkable way. In that instant he beheld the mystery of the world. He attempted to stop the vision, but the more he tried the clearer his sight became. He went out and walked along the street seeking to escape the things he saw. For seven days and nights he struggled against the mysterious force that moved within him, but it was useless. The lightning flash had struck, the eyes of the seer were opened, and he was moved by a power far greater than himself.

Having finished his apprenticeship Boehme settled in Gorlitz as a master shoemaker, and was appointed his proper seat in the local church. Here he partook regularly of the Lord's Supper, and affirmed his obedience to the covenants of the Church. He took to wife Katharina, the beloved daughter of Hans Kuntzschmann, the local butcher. Four sons graced this union, of whom three survived their father. For thirty years, until his death, Boehme lived happily with his wife and family, and there is no report that any discord existed among them.

Boehme plied his trade industriously and successfully for ten years, at the end of which time he purchased a good house in the Neisee-Vorstadt. Soon afterward he gave up his profession, probably because his health was impaired by the cramped position in which shoemakers did their work. He then began the manufacture of woolen gloves, and made an annual trip to Prague to sell them at the local fair.

It is difficult to assign to Boehme his proper place in the world of mystical philosophy. The title 'theosophist' has been applied to him to distinguish his method from that usual to seers. He did not converse with the spirits of the departed, and he beheld no blessed vision of the gods. Unlike Swedenborg, he did not fraternize with the angels, and no spiritualistic or psychic phenomena was present. He practiced no divination, nor did he prepare himself by the aid of esoteric rituals or self-discipline. Unlike most mystics, he was not seeking personal contentment, and he did not retire from the world to solitary communion with God. His own humility was the magic key that opened for him the kingdom of the spirit.

In one of his writings Boehme refers to Moses and the prophets of old. He explained that these men spoke not their own words nor the words of their minds. When they delivered their instructions they first said, "So sayeth the Lord." Of himself Boehme would say, "Man speaks not of the mysteries of the spirit; rather it is God, who alone knows all things, that speaks through the lips of man."

Boehme's mystical seership took the form of an unfoldment of God through nature before his eyes. He beheld, as one present, the working of the law. First was the *Ungrund,* the abyss, the nothing and all, time and eternity. Here dwelt the Eternal One, solitary but never alone. From the *Ungrund* came forth the powers, the seven eternal qualities that forever change and yet forever are the same. First came desire, and from desire motion, and from motion anguish, the great disquietude. Here dwells the eternal hunger which calls forth the flash of lightning, the spirit of God. This lightning illumines and sustains the love-fire from which comes forth sound, which is the voice of the silence. These are contained as in a cup by the body of God, which is called nature, or the essential wisdom.

Is it to be wondered that only a few have been able to understand the obscure writings of the German theosopher? His words are strange, for he gathered them from a variety of sources but used them in a manner all his own. He knew that the visions which he recorded could be understood by only those who shared the vision. To the profane the strange sayings would be meaningless, but God through him had revealed them, and God in another man could understand them.

Although Boehme began his mystical examination into the secrets of nature about the year 1600, he made no effort to record his experiences until ten years later. Then fearing that his memory might fail him in some of the details, he resolved to preserve his findings in a private diary. With considerable difficulty because of his lack of schooling, he wrote out the principles of his philosophy. Some friends assisted in the selecting of terms, but in many cases their help, though well-intended, confused the issues.

Early biographers agree that Boehme wrote without the aid of any reference books except the Holy Bible. It is likely that some of the more learned of his acquaintances were the sources of his alchemical, cabalistic, and hermetic terms and symbols. His own humility of mind caused him to accept eagerly all suggestions, and he was in desperate need of some kind of terminology. It was probably his selection of words rather than the substance of his ideas that resulted in his conflict with the Lutheran Church.

In the year 1612 Boehme completed his first book, which he called *Morning Redness at Sunrise*. Dr. Balthazar Walter suggested the name Aurora as a proper word to cover

Boehme's meaning, and the book was later issued as *Aurora*. For some time the author kept the manuscript to himself, permitting only a few of his friends to glimpse its contents. The writing came to the attention of an enthusiastic devotee by the name of Karl von Ender. After much persuasion he succeeded in borrowing the original that he might peruse it at greater leisure. The moment he got it home he made a complete copy, bringing in several professional scriveners to hasten the work. He in turn showed his new treasure to those in sympathy with Boehme's growing reputation as a mystic. Finally the writing came to the attention of Parson Richter, and trouble resulted.

The word Richter in German means a judge, and the Pastor Primarius appointed himself a tribunal of one to defend the city of Gorlitz from the dangerous heresy of its principal shoemaker. He denounced Boehme from the pulpit with language more fitted to the tap-room than the house of God. But the stolid citizens were so accustomed to the preacher's pious rages that the sermon failed to stir them appropriately. Richter, not to be discouraged by public apathy, included a vicious attack upon Boehme in each of his Sunday sermons thereafter. Throughout his campaign of attack and denunciation Boehme attended church regularly and listened quietly and humbly to the ravings of the clergyman. At no time did he utter a complaint or protest.

At last the parson's fanatical fury exhausted the patience of the entire community, and that Right Worshipful and Celebrated group which made up the city council held a special session with the 'truly sapient' burgomaster to end the squabbling. The local government did not dare to ignore the complaint of the representative of the local Lutheran clergy. On the other hand they had no particular desire to persecute their fellow citizen. They called Boehme before them, confiscated his manuscript, and asked him in the cause of common peace to discontinue his mystical writings. They further recommended that he content himself with his highly respected trade of master shoemaker and leave the mysteries of God to Parson Richter.

For seven years thereafter Boehme bowed to the will of the city council and discontinued writing. During this time Richter's watchful eye was upon him, but the clergyman could find nothing in the quiet life of the shoemaker upon which he could bring censure. Richter was uneasy, however, for he could see that the better minds of the community were more and more sympathetic to Boehme's visions. A full-sized heresy was in the making, and it was up to the clergy to destroy its roots.

It was not until 1619 that Boehme resumed his writing. He was inspired by the entreaties of his friends and the sincere conviction that his mystical doctrines should be preserved for posterity. Having decided on this course of action he devoted most of his time to his books, indifferent of the attacks made upon his person and doctrines by the clergy. In 1623 Abraham von Frankenberg arranged for the publication of several of Boehme's shorter writings under the title *The Way to Christ*. It was the only book that appeared in print during the lifetime of the author. Parson Richter's rage reached apoplectic proportions. An ignorant shoemaker had dared to write a religious book without the approval of the clergy.

Richter prepared a pasquinade against Boehme. This was a form of broadside, a short writing of condemnation and ridicule which he posted like a handbill in various public places. Richter's use of profanity from the pulpit was a scandal to his church, and it was feared that the clergy might bring pressure by appealing to the lord elector of Saxony.

Boehme made a personal appeal to Richter. The clergyman was seated in his study and was so infuriated by the mere presence of the mystic that he threw one of his boots at him. Boehme quietly picked it up and placed it with the other beside the clergyman's chair. He humbly requested that Richter specify his accusations and tell in what way he had by word or action departed from the Christian way of life. Richter was not able to present one particular complaint; he merely resorted to blind rage.

Boehme presented a simple petition to the city council asking protection against Richter's unsupported accusations. The council reminded Boehme of the power of the clergy and the probability of its entire machinery being turned against him if Richter continued. They advised him to leave the community for his own good, as it was still possible that he might be tried for heresy and be burned at the stake. His own influence was not great enough to protect him, and the government would be likely to appease the clergy. It was good advice in those days and given in all kindness, and Boehme decided to comply lest the whole community suffer.

In May 1624 Boehme went to Dresden where he was received into the home of a prominent physician, Dr. Benjamin Hinkelman. While there he was requested by the emperor to take part in a discussion with several learned theologians and mathematicians relating to his mystical doctrine. It was a veiled effort to investigate the nature of the difficulties at Gorlitz. At this session the simple, unlearned shoemaker completely dumfounded the theologians with his insight into the mysteries of faith. Their conclusion was that they could pass no judgment without a long period of time in which to study the opinions that the shoemaker so admirably and yet so humbly advanced and maintained. One of the group, Dr. Gerhard, said that he would not take the whole world as a bribe to condemn such a man, and another savant, Dr. Meissner, stated that he was of the same mind. Thus it is evident that the whole clergy was in no way of the temper of Parson Richter. The emperor was deeply impressed, and Boehme was free of any danger that the state would move against him.

Parson Richter died in August, 1624, a frustrated old man full of venom. With his pertinacious foe out of the way Boehme could look forward to peace and security, but his own life was strangely linked with that of his enemy. He was stricken with a fever, and was brought back to Gorlitz to die. With his permission the Reverend Elias Theodorus was summoned, and he grudgingly consented to question Boehme in theology to the end of administering the Lord's Supper. Boehme died on Sunday, the 17th of November, 1624, just before the time of the opening of the city gates. At two o'clock in the morning he asked the hour, and when told replied, "In three hours will be my time." He asked his son Tobias if he could hear the beautiful music that filled the room, but the young man shook his head. A little later Boehme talked with his wife, instructing her in the disposition of his manuscripts and belongings. He also told her that she would not long survive him, which proved to be true. Having ordered all of his earthly affairs and taken leave of his sons, he asked the eldest to turn him on the bed. His last words were, "Now I shall enter the paradise."

After Boehme's death a serious crisis arose, due to the pressure of the clergy. His body was refused decent Christian burial, and it was necessary for the widow to appeal twice to

the city council for the disposal of the remains. The timely
arrival of the Catholic Count Hannival von Drohna saved
the situation. He ordered that the body be buried with all
solemnity in the presence of two members of the city council,
that there be a procession, that the clergy be represented, and
that there be the usual sermon in the local church. As an
excuse for not attending, the principal parson took a large
dose of laxative, but there is no evidence that it purged him
of his intolerance.

When the time came for the sermon the minister prefaced
his remarks with an elaborate defense of his own position.
He assured the congregation that he was preaching under
pressure and had no pleasure in the task. He also stated ex-
plicitly that he had refused the usual fee lest he be suspected
of having preached for gain. Later, however, he billed the
widow. The sermon consisted of a halfhearted Christian
hope that Boehme might escape the full measure of perdition
because of the infinite forgiveness of God which might extend even to heretics. A curious symbolic cross supplied by
friends in distant places was raised over the grave. This,
however, was later destroyed by vandalism, and it is the sober
judgment of the ages that the Church made no great effort
to preserve the monument.

Thus ended the physical life of Jakob Boehme, citizen of
Gorlitz and master shoemaker. He lived and died plagued
by the intemperance of little minds. He is a proof that ideas
are imperishable, and extending beyond their narrow origin
can exercise a profound effect in far times and distant places.

It is practically impossible to digest the writings of Boehme
in anything resembling his own words, yet the mystical
philosophy which he taught is in substance quite simple. As
he himself said: "My writings are for only those who are will-

ing to receive the truth in a simple and childlike state of mind, for it is they who are to possess the kingdom of God. I have written for only those that seek; to the cunning and the worldly-wise I have nothing to say."

According to Sigmund Freud, religion is a kind of neurosis, an escape from truth along pleasant avenues of self-delusion. The human being, afraid to face the reality of his own unimportance and impermanence, prefers a fairy tale to the testimony of his reason and the senses. Freud is inclined to believe that the whole world would be better off if men became realists, and he regards realism as an indication of intellectual maturity.

Is it possible that Freud has confused religion and theology? As regards theology, most of his points are well-taken, but as to religion, man's timeless search for God and good, perhaps the father of modern psychology is not completely informed. Certainly the mystical experience as it came to Jakob Boehme is not an ordinary consequence of neurosis or frustration. Nor can we regard as illusions those inner happenings which lift man from the commonplace to the estate of philosopher by the strength of inner consciousness alone.

The Boehmenists, as the followers of Boehme were called in England and Holland, exercised considerable influence over the religious thought of their time. Most of them merged into the Quaker and the Friends movements. The Philadelphian Society of the early 18th century included several important mystics who had been nourished upon the teachings of Boehme. The Pietists who came to America in the closing years of the 17th century brought many of Boehme's writings with them, and were much given to his kind of metaphysical thought.

After Boehme's death one of the leading exponents of his
system was Johann Georg Gichtel, a man possessing considerable insight and mystical powers. In 1682 he republished
the master's writings, adding to the text many curious symbolical engravings now highly valued. Gichtel suffered much
persecution and was several times imprisoned for his part in
spreading Boehmenism. He formed a society called the
Brethern of the Angels, which was devoted to good work and
the practice of Christian charity. It was his hope that the
brothers of his order would sometime replace the priesthood,
and free human society from the burden of the clergy.

There is much in the symbolism of Boehme that is reminiscent of the teachings of the Gnostics. Gnosticism arose in
both Syria and Egypt about the middle of the 1st century.
It taught a system of emanations as a solution to the problem
of spirit and matter. Pure spirit and pure matter cannot
mingle unless they are brought together in some common
medium. Spirit emanates from itself an order of descending
qualities, and matter emanates a corresponding series of ascending qualities. These finally unite in a middle distance, thus
binding the extremes into world harmony. A number of
Gichtel's drawings illustrate the doctrine of emanation as the
only means of reconciling the mystery of eternity and time.

Although Boehme's writings never depart from the word
of the Scriptures, his interpretation shows little theological
influence. He finds a mystical depth in every verse of the
Scriptures. Thus the Bible cannot be read; it must be experienced. Unless the light of God illumines the words there is
only darkness. This darkness is a perplexity of the reason,
the root of doubts, and the source of endless controversy.
Boehme was one of the first to point out that religion is not
an unreasonable veneration of history. Man finds consolation

not from the account of deeds performed in the distant past, but from the eternal verities for which these historical incidents are merely symbols. Devotion to God is not to be attained by a defense of the written letter of his law, but by a personal participation in that law by mystical communion.

The Mysterium Magnum

The beginning of Boehme's philosophy is the mystery of the abyss, the nothing and the all, the absolute nature of God. Deity is neither person nor thing, neither beginning nor end, but the *mysterium magnum*. The nature of the abyss is unknown and unknowable save by itself, and all efforts to describe its qualities can be only allegories and symbols.

Concealed within the abyss, as time is concealed within eternity, is the uncreated will which Boehme calls the byss— that which ever desires to be something. These two, byss and abyss, are together the hidden cause. It is the byss, or will of the Supreme One, that fashions the mirror of the world in which it may perceive by reflection all of the wonders that lie latent in the abyss. Boehme did not believe with the theologians that the universe was fashioned from nothing; rather, it was the thing formed from the no-thing, the formless, by the power of the will.

The abyss was a great richness or fullness, like a dark earth full of seed from which all things can grow. Within the abyss is an infinite nutrition—the infinite mother that can nourish the seeds of life which are the will of the father. Creation is therefore a motion toward manifestation of things hidden in the will of God.

From the abyss shines forth the three principles. The first two abide as one and are named fire and light, or wrath and mercy. Wrath is law, and mercy is love, and from the union of these two is born nature, the child of law and love. Fire is the dark principle in God. This is a great mystery, for the dark fire if left closed is good, but if opened becomes evil. Let us try to understand what Boehme means by his strange terms. All nature is subject to the law of God; the law is invisible but everywhere present, and by its own nature it requires obedience from all its creations. If these creatures depart from the law they open the door of its wrath and the will of God becomes an instrument of punishment.

One of the old Greek legislators, in describing the man-made laws governing nations, explained that those who obey the statutes are unaware of their existence, but those who disobey immediately feel their weight. This is what Boehme is trying to tell us. All suffering, sin, and death, result from disobedience by which the fire of God is revealed as wrath or punishment.

God does not will that the door of wrath be opened, but he permits it to be opened in order that his creatures may be self-knowing. Man cannot experience the love of God without knowing of the anguish. In other words, no one can be good without knowledge of the existence of evil. The door of wrath is opened by the self-will of man, which is in conflict with the divine will. Yet self-will will be necessary; otherwise the power of the divine will could never be known in the creature. Self-will is the dark principle natural to God, but unnatural to man. It is by self-will that Deity formed the world, and in Deity this will is law, but when man attempts the power of God by opposing his self-will to the self-will of the Infinite, law becomes wrath in his heart and false imagination is born.

Creation is an unfolding of the seven eternal qualities from within outwardly, like the opening of the petals of a flower. An order of spheres and worlds is born out of each other and are given their places in space. Each of these dominions is fertile with life and generates creatures in an infinite diversity. Yet in this diversity there is no conflict, no discord, and all abide together 'in temperature.' This temperature is the harmony of the divine will which moves all things by the law of the dark principle.

Boehme especially mentioned an angelic world in which are placed three hierarchs—Michael, Lucifer, and Uriel. In the world of the angels Michael represents God the Father, Lucifer, God the Son, and Uriel, God the Holy Spirit.

The Fall of Lucifer

Boehme's explanation of the fall of Lucifer and the rebellion of the angels is one of the most daring and remarkable of his doctrines. Here it is especially necessary to read between the lines and sense a mystery in the spirit. Lucifer turned his face toward the throne of God and beheld not grandeur but humility. He saw not a great king ruling over all creations, but an infinite gentleness, quiet, silent, and alone. This prince of the angels had not the mysticism in his own heart to examine the infinite love and patience of the Creator. So he opened the door of wrath, that he might know the power of the Infinite. The harmony of the worlds had never known the wrath of God until Lucifer was moved by the lust for knowledge. But as self-will entered into him the very throne of the Father changed before his eyes. The gentleness vanished, the humility was gone, and the patience had come to an end. The light of God was revealed as a consuming fire. Suddenly Lucifer beheld the Supreme in all the magnificence of the avenger. This was not because God had changed, but because Lucifer had changed. The gentleness, humility, and patience were in reality still there, but the rebel angel could no longer see them; he had obscured the will of God in himself and self-will came in its place. It was thus that the door of wrath was opened and the material centrum was set up in the abyss.

Here Boehme reveals the essential doctrine of mysticism by contrasting consciousness and intellect. The spiritual eye which perceives the humility of God is consciousness, but the mental power which is aware only of the splendor of God as revealed through the creation is the intellect.

Lucifer was resolved to create a kingdom more glorious than that of the Father. This kingdom should be filled with knowledge, wealth, power, and ambition. He would become a conqueror of space, and the sciences should be the instruments of his achievement. He would prove the power of might over right, and his motto was "I can do anything that I will to do." His body became the physical world and his children became mankind resolved to conquer all things by will and intellect. This is the true meaning of the building of the Tower of Babel. In the end was confusion and chaos, which Boehme calls the *turba,* the self-will manifested as many self-wills set up against each other. Each man defended his own errors and fought for his opinions. The result was a discord of races, nations, sciences, philosophies, and theologies. In all of them men were fighting not for truth but for opinion. Thus vanished the harmony of the angels. They knew but one will and they dwelt in peace. Men have many wills, and they dwell in confusion.

In the mysticism of Boehme, Adam was not regarded as a man but as a kind of spiritual creation which dwelt in the love and light of divine humility. Within Adam like a seed was his own external nature, his physical body or coat of skins. One old Bible refers to Adam's body as 'a pair of breeches.' This indicates to some degree how far the translators departed from the mystical implications of the text. The spiritual Adam was also androgynous (both male and female) and the mystery of Eve was still locked within him.

The fall of Lucifer was repeated in Adam, with one difference. Lucifer set up his will in direct opposition to God with full knowledge of the consequences, but Adam was without malice, seeking only for experience. Within Adam, Michael the power of God, and Lucifer the power of self-will, dwell in eternal conflict. When Adam permitted his imagination to be directed toward material things a sleep descended upon his spirit. As Boehme says, "He fell asleep to the angelical world, and awakened to the external world." Truth is unity; error is diversity. When Adam became aware of diversity he knew his own duality, and Eve came into being and stood before him out of himself.

Adam and Eve, the archetypes of all species, first dwelt together in the Garden of Eden, which is the sphere of the ethers. Later, in the search for self-knowing, they descended into the deepest parts of matter. This was the involution, and the struggle of mankind to escape from the material principle is the true evolution.

The Mystical Union with Christ

Christ is the second Adam. In him is accomplished the conquest of wrath. The initiate Jesus centered his imagination entirely upon the humility of the Father. By this mystery he vanquished the self-will and became greater than death. Jesus looked upon the wrath of the Father, that is, the law, and perceived in it the secret of the love principle. In that instant he stood before the gentleness of God, which is eternal within and behind the wrath.

The true Christ is the love of God which is born in the heart of man as Jesus was born in a stable surrounded by animals—symbols of the self-will. Although Boehme insisted on the historical fact of Christ, he also pointed out the significance of the Messiah as the mystical experience. The historical Christ could not insure the salvation of man; only the Christ within could be the hope of glory. The seed of Christ is in every human heart. If man nourishes this seed it will grow into a great tree and its fruits will be peace and everlasting life. Christ comes for the healing of the sickness of Lucifer and the redemption of the first Adam who fell into the illusion.

The way of mystical union is through the heart of man to the heart of Christ. In this heart is the eye which may look upon the gentleness of the Father. The opening of this eye is the mystical experience of faith. When this eye is opened the empire of self-will, ruled over by the fallen angel, vanishes. There is no longer confusion or doubt about things human and divine. There is simple faith and complete submission to the dark principle which is the law of the Father. The eye of the mystic can look upon the silence of the throne and rejoice in the meekness which Lucifer despised.

Such in substance is the vision of Jakob Boehme, and all his philosophy extends from this central theme. A child becomes a man by the increase of self-will, but the man becomes a child again by the miracle of faith. Strength gives place to beauty, the greater strength. Courage gives place to obedience, which requires the greater courage. Aspiration ends in peace, the end which all ambitions vainly seek. The world is dissolved in God, who is the greater world.

The effect of Boehme's writings extended in many directions. The English mystic, William Law, noted that Sir Isaac Newton was a diligent student of Boehme's writings, and among Newton's papers were found copious extracts carefully copied in his own handwriting. The extracts are especially numerous in a tract in which Sir Isaac appeals to all who doubt or disbelieve the truths of the Gospel. Newton's scientific standing makes these extracts all the more remarkable.

According to Dr. Law the English King, Charles I, was an earnest reader and admirer of Boehme, and sent a well-qualified person from England to Gorlitz to acquire the German language and to collect every anecdote he could meet with that was relative to this great mystic.

An effort has been made to identify Jakob Boehme with the Rosicrucians, a sect which was developed in the opening quarter of the 17th century. But careful investigation does not sustain this opinion. Although Boehme was later identified with the Rosicrucians principally because of his symbols and diagrams, there is no proof that he was actually connected with the society at any time. He was self-taught, and it is impossible to explain away his revelations by attributing them to outside influences.

It may be useful to compare Boehme briefly with two other mystics who have a particular claim for consideration. It should be remembered that while the structure of a mystical revelation is strongly influenced by external circumstances, the spiritual content is ever the same.

Baron Emanuel Swedenborg

Baron Emanuel Swedenborg (1688-1772) was a man of profound erudition and outstanding scientific attainments. He wrote on a variety of subjects and attained prominence in mathematics, invention, astronomy, chemistry, anatomy, and physiology. One of his most practical contributions was a cure for smoky chimneys. In his spare time he designed the plans for a flying machine.

Swedenborg enjoyed the respect, admiration, and fraternity of prominent thinkers, statesmen, and scientists. He was ennobled by Queen Ulrika Eleanora in 1719, and was offered chairs in prominent universities. He was fifty-seven when the mystical experience occurred to him which was to completely change the course of his life. The details are not preserved, but it appears that his illumination resulted especially from his mathematical speculations.

For some years prior to his illumination Swedenborg had received visions and heard the voices of invisible beings. He had resolved to attempt the discovery of God by scientific means, and had made elaborate studies of anatomy and physiology in an effort to isolate the spiritual energy at the source of human life. He knew of the works of Pythagoras, Paracelsus, and Boehme, and there are indications that he had some acquaintance with the mystical philosophies of the Far East. All together he was a remarkable man.

According to Swedenborg's own account God appeared to him in a revelation saying, "I have chosen thee to unfold the spiritual sense of the Holy Scripture. I will myself dictate to you what thou shalt write." Swedenborg was a voluminous scribe, and in the last twenty-seven years of his

life authored nearly forty books. He traveled extensively, and
to the end of his life remained interested in a variety of subjects, although his mystical writings were his principal concern.

In Swedenborg's teachings the substance of God is infinite
love, and his manifestation is infinite wisdom. As the physical sun lights the material world, so a spiritual sun is the
source of love and intelligence. In fact, the material sun receives its appearance of life from the spiritual orb behind it.
Human consciousness seeking truth rises through an order
of spheres or conditions of understanding. Through the
virtue of mystical love man attunes himself with ever higher
aspects of the divine nature.

In Swedenborg's writings, thought spiritualized by understanding so that it becomes wisdom is far more important
than in the teachings of Boehme. This is only natural when
we realize that Swedenborg was a trained thinker. He was
able to see the mystery of love in the sciences, and to regard
knowledge as being equal to faith as a means of salvation.

In his personal life Swedenborg was by nature kind and
generous. He lived modestly, and his food consisted principally of bread, milk, and coffee. It was his habit to remain
in a state of trance for several days at a time, and occasionally
he would have terrifying ordeals with demons.

One of the central ideas of Swedenborg's system of mystical philosophy was his doctrine of correspondences. Each
visible thing has an appropriate spiritual reality associated
with it. This agrees with the teachings of Paracelsus and
Boehme regarding signatures. Forms are symbols of principles, and the receptacles of divine energy.

The clairvoyance of Swedenborg took the form of journeys
into the world of spirit, and conversations with the creatures

who dwelt there. He approached his subject as scientifically as the nature of the factors would permit. He allowed no mystical exaltation to interfere with his judgment. In defending his method he wrote: "I have proceeded by observation and induction as strict as that of any man of science among you. Only it has been given me to enjoy and experience reaching into two worlds—that of spirit as well as that of matter." He regarded his method as more certain than that of other mystics because he depended not upon the experiences of consciousness alone, but upon the testimony of extrasensory perception.

In his writing Swedenborg clearly revealed his scientific training. He proceeds as a practiced observer, without emotion and with great attention to detail. He notes that in the language of the angels only vowels are used because these are the spiritual parts of words. Yet when they addressed him these beings spoke to his inner understanding in the language of mortals. If, however, they turned to address each other they used a method of communication so subtle that the seer heard no sound.

The writings of Swedenborg include a description of the creatures inhabiting the various planets. His remarks on this subject can be estimated from the following quotation: "The inhabitants of the moon are small, like children six or seven years old; at the same time they have the strength of men like ourselves. Their voice rolls like thunder, and the sound proceeds from the belly because the moon is in quite a different atmosphere from the other planets."

The presentation of such material by a quiet, scholarly old gentleman with a powdered wig neatly curled on the ends was the cause of considerable consternation. Some opined that the Baron had overtaxed his mind and was suffering from delusions, yet all acknowledged that he retained full control of his reasoning faculties and his scientific method never failed. Never before, however, had science been applied to such a variety of abstract intangibles.

It was Swedenborg's desire to establish a new church. This church could include all others without interfering with any of the existing creeds. Swedenborgianism has exercised a considerable influence and has many followers in the modern world. Samuel Coleridge, Robert and Elizabeth Browning, and Thomas Carlyle imbibed inspiration from him, and Helen Keller has found great comfort in the Swedenborgian faith.

Nineteenth-century mysticism mingled its stream with the current of New England spiritualism. As a result a quantity of psychical phenomena is present in the popular metaphysics of today. Communication with the dead became an end in itself, and the abstract philosophical side of mysticism received little attention. It is a mistake to regard mysticism and psychism as synonymous terms, but psychism is in some respects a scientific approach to the mysteries of the invisible world.

Andrew Jackson Davis, the Seer of Poughkeepsie

The transition from mysticism to psychism is clearly shown in the writings of the American seer Andrew Jackson Davis (1826-1910). Davis not only derived part of his teachings from Swedenborg, but believed that he was in direct communication with the spirit of the great Swedish mystic. Davis had very little formal education, and began his literary career when he was about sixteen. He attended some lectures on hypnotism and animal magnetism, and discovered that he possessed the power of healing the sick. Soon afterwards he began receiving spirit messages, and dictated several books while in the state of trance. He was involved in psychic phenomena before the official founding of modern spiritualism, and identified himself with the movement about 1850. In all, he was the author of about thirty books, of which the best known is *The Great Harmonia* in six volumes.

It has been said that the inspiration behind the writings of Davis was literary rather than truly mystical. Those who have read his works, however, realize that mysticism played an important part in the shaping of his viewpoint. He was essentially a teacher, and his writings abound in practical applications, especially in the fields of morality and health.

Davis was known among his associates as the Seer of Poughkeepsie. Like Boehme he was self-taught, but he never penetrated deeply into the *Mysterium Magnum* as did the German theosophist. He depended upon the older mystics for the general conception of the invisible world, and concerned himself primarily with the motions of spiritual force in the physical life of man.

A number of mystical organizations rose to prominence between 1840 and 1880. Their rise corresponded to the increased interest that was centering on the development of the physical sciences. A wave of materialism was sweeping across the world, and the natural mysticism everywhere present in human nature rose to oppose the opinions of Darwin and Huxley. Unfortunately, the popular mysticism of the present century lacks true devotional content. Would-be mystics are dabbling in old doctrines as an intellectual pastime. For this reason it is important that the teachings of the older mystics such as Meister (Johannes) Eckhart, Jan van Ruysbroeck, and Louis Claude de Saint-Martin be made available to the truth

seekers of the present day. Mysticism has a great and noble
tradition and has always been a constructive force in society.
It teaches tolerance, brotherhood, and the practice of good
works.

Prominent among Occidental mystics stands Jakob
Boehme, and no other philosopher more perfectly portrays
the virtues of the mystical life. In the years that lie ahead,
years burdened with the responsibility of building an enduring cultural system, mysticism will have an important part
to play. More and more the world must be guided by the
mystic impulses which come through the heart of man.

6

THE MESSIAH OF PURE REASON

IMMANUEL KANT

German Philosophy

GERMAN philosophy had its beginning with Gottfried
Wilhelm von Leibnitz (1646-1716). He was an idealist
deeply influenced by classical philosophy and the atomic
theory of Democritus, the laughing philosopher (late 5th and
early 4th century B. C.) Leibnitz was a philosophical cosmop-
olite; he was interested in everything that could add to the
substance of his understanding. He read the books of the
classical Greeks, the Alexandrian Neoplatonists, the Egyptian
hermetists, the Jewish cabalists, the early Christian patristics,
and the medieval scholastics.

By nature optimistic and idealistic, Baron von Leibnitz
saw good in all the systems and sensed the need of a common
denominator by which diverse opinions could be bound
together for purposes of utility. To this end he recommended
the establishment of a learned society where intellectuals could
gather and benefit by a mutual exchange of ideas. He also
suggested that it might be advisable to create a philosophical

IMMANUEL KANT

language composed of ideographic symbols in order that thinkers might have a speech in common.

The principal contribution of Leibnitz, written in what he called 'odd moments', was his doctrine of monads, which he borrowed directly from the old Greeks. Matter reduced to its ultimate form and most minute particles ceases to exist as a physical substance, being resolved in a mass of nonmaterial ideas or metaphysical units of power, which Leibnitz called monads. The universe is composed of an infinite number of these monads, which are like seeds and capable of eternal growth. God is the first and greatest of the monads.

The Neoplatonic speculations of Leibnitz intrigued the mind of Immanuel Kant and transformed the little professor of Konigsberg from a schoolmaster into a philosopher. But before we enter into a discussion of Kant it is important to make a brief survey of the workings of the German mind in the world of abstract thinking.

Prior to the time of Kant the Teutonic states had developed a curious neurosis as the result of a long series of military reverses. This neurosis has influenced the entire school of German intellectuals for the past three hundred years. As a result two streams of ideology have run parallel in the German mind. One school was composed of exact thinkers leaning heavily upon mathematics as the basis of reason. The other school verged toward psychological romanticism and the deification of the German volk (folk), and the justification of militarism as the proper purpose of life. The divergence of these two schools is exemplified in the attack made by Werner Sombart in 1915 upon Kant's book on perpetual peace. Sombart called the writing a wretched book and an inglorious exception to Kant's genius, on the ground that no representative German had ever been guilty of uttering a

pacifist statement. While Professor Sombart may or may not
be a representative German, the antagonism between the two
schools is revealed in its usual form.

Nietzsche was a prominent exponent of the volk psychology, yet both he and Kant were deeply influenced by Neoplatonism. It was a matter of interpretation. It is very easy
for mysticism to lead toward romanticism, which is a metaphysical escape from reality. When Kant attacked the concept of a personal God he weakened the idealism of his time.
There was no longer any religious limitation upon human
behavior. The simple Christian virtues of gentleness, humility,
and faith had less meaning if the Christian way of life was an
illusion. Thus Kant, probably without the slightest realization of what he was doing, prepared the way for Nietzsche's
superman and all its consequences.

The Oracle of Konigsberg

A little man sat hunched up behind his desk in the University of Konigsberg. He wore a powdered periwig with the
curls precisely over each ear. His coat was plain and slightly
open at the neck to show a proper stock, but the coat buttons
were large and not exactly in the best of taste. With big
blue eyes that always held a look of wonder he gazed out
into an eager sea of faces. Carefully and methodically he
drew from his inside pocket a number of small slips of paper.
These he arranged in orderly rows on the desk before him.
Then reaching over he hesitated for a moment. Yes, this
morning he would use five books, no more, no less. These
he opened one by one to passages previously marked. The
books were then arranged in a neat pattern, and the little
man surveyed his accomplishments as though he doubted the

exactness of his method. The assembled students remained
in silent awe; the time had come for the oracle to speak.

The oracle was Herr Professor Doctor Immanuel Kant,
and his classroom was the shrine of universal learning. Never
before had so much mentality been wrapped up in so small
and neat a package. The messiah of pure reason to whom
all mysteries were open books always began his lecture at
the mathematical moment for which it was scheduled; never
a second early, never a second late.

The little man's voice was appropriate to his size. It was
very feeble, high-pitched, and interrupted by frequent pauses
as though he lacked the strength to continue. Perfect silence
was necessary in order that his words might be heard. Nor
should we imagine that this was Kant in the feebleness of his
declining years; this was the great professor in his prime
when the intellectuals of Europe prostrated themselves before
his low, well-worn desk.

As the lecture proceeded the wonder grew. To read Kant
is to labor not only with the profundity of his ideas, but the
ponderosity of his style. His books groan with the burden
of his words, and only the most courageous explore the writings beyond the introductory pages. But Kant the lecturer
was an entirely different person. His sentences were short
and well-turned. There were numerous interesting anecdotes,
observations, and familiar illustrations. He never read his
lectures, but cast an occasional furtive glance at the tidy rows
of notes as though he disliked to be suspected of referring to
them. As the lecture proceeded the professor became more
and more emotionally involved. These talks were probably
the only emotional experiences in his well-regulated life.
His small voice became positively eloquent, and his listeners
were carried away by the magic of his thoughts.

At the exact moment when a lecture should end the discourse was finished. It was always neatly finished, the notes carefully put away, and the five books returned to their proper places. Then the little man with the big, wondering eyes became entirely oblivious of the student body, and prepared for the next part of his daily routine. His formula for teaching was simple. Always address your remarks to the intermediate level of your listeners. The geniuses will take care of themselves, and the dunces are beyond human remedy.

The temperament of Immanuel Kant was a combination of stolid Scotch ancestry on one side and stolid Prussian ancestry on the other. He looked enough like Frederick the Great to be his brother, and all the burden of his thought had to be carried by a body scarcely five feet tall. Small men are given to certainties and large projects. Kant was certain that his philosophy was the proper end of all philosophy. There could be nothing added to his revelation by the future. He grew decidedly irritable if anyone suggested that posterity might improve upon his method. For the largeness of his project it need only be said that his task was to put the entire universe in order. There were no lose ends in learning when he finished tucking them into place. He was born into a world heavily laden with opinion. After his advent humanity would be divided into only two groups; those supremely ignorant and those who studied Kant. There was no egotism in the little man; he simply knew that he was right. Whether the Scottish or Prussian ancestry nourished this conviction we cannot know.

Some have hinted that Kant was slightly deficient in the region of his sentiments. Of course a man burdened with a cosmic responsibility can be forgiven if he lives with his mind pretty much on the subject. The Herr Professor had no appreciation of art as a source of emotional pleasure, but he could circumscribe it with an all-embracing critique. A sunset left him entirely unmoved, and for travel he had no mind at all. Music was noise, and poetry nothing but jogging prose that trotted along with little influence on the ultimate destiny of human nature. Goethe and Schiller might think they were philosophers, but men who dealt in verses could not be sound thinkers. As for the female sex, Kant sort of forgot them. His philosophy worked very well without the feminine equation, so why bring in irrelevancies. He never married; in fact it was unthinkable that so methodical a person should allow matrimony to interfere with his daily schedule. Yet he was a friendly man as long as friendship remained dignified and emotionless. To worry about friends interfered with his continuity of thought, and if one of his acquaintances became ill he studiously avoided him. Death was another annoying sentiment, and it was generally understood that no mention of a deceased acquaintance should be made in his presence. The good professor must have been a very emotional man or it would not have been necessary to maintain such a defensive armament.

Immanuel Kant was born at Konigsberg on the 22nd of April, 1724. His father was a saddle maker, and both of his parents were members of a strict sect of Christian mystics which flourished in that part of Germany. Kant never ceased to wonder at the effect of religion in the life of his home. As he grew older he lost all sympathy with the creed of his family, but retained a deep respect for the spiritual integrity which it produced in the characters of his parents.

Influenced no doubt by his home environment, young Immanuel was but ten when he began his schooling preparatory to majoring in theology. Later his mind turned toward mathematics, but he continued his religious studies and even preached an occasional sermon. From childhood ill health played an important part in his life. He was frail and ailing, and further handicapped by a deformity of the right shoulder. Periodically he would collapse from no particular ailment, and often his life seemed destined to end prematurely. Then there were long periods of recuperation which interfered with his struggle for an education. As he grew older he realized that he must set his mind toward preserving his body or he would never be able to accomplish his goal — a professorship in the University of Konigsberg.

His early experiences with physicians did not increase his confidence in the medical profession, so he came to the decision that the first law of health was to keep away from doctors. During his entire lifetime it was his boast that in his mature years he had never gone to a doctor, no matter how grievous his illness. He lived by the sheer force of will, and in one of his essays he discusses the power of will and purpose over the limitations of the flesh. His training in mathematics and his intense desire to extend his life resulted in the completely ordered existence for which he was famous.

Kant never broke a habit nor deviated from one in the slightest degree. He believed, for example, that for the sake of health he should always breathe through his nostrils when walking out of doors. As a consequence he would not speak to his best friend if he chanced to meet him on the street because it would necessitate opening his mouth. If he had met the king face to face he would not have spoken; a rule is a rule.

The little professor also maintained that a man's life, to be long, must be regular. At that time coffee was one of the elegancies, a luxury that few could indulge in, but Kant had one cup of coffee at exactly the same time every day for forty-six years. He went for a walk every afternoon at three-thirty, and the neighbors set their clocks by him.

During the entire period of his professorship Kant was never known to be a little early or a little late to a meal, and there is no record that he ever performed a spontaneous action. Naturally, such rigid self-discipline depressed the romantic side of his life. It is said that he twice fell in love, a state of mind and heart that threatened to interfere with his prescribed routine. He was so hesitant about changing his ways that the first young lady married someone else while he was weighing the values involved. The second object of his affections he considered seriously for a period of about ten years, but she finally moved away. The difficulty seemed to hinge upon his food habits; he always ate at a certain time, and any interference with this rhythm would be extremely serious.

In all probability Kant suffered from a deep-seated inferiority complex. Physically small and weak, he was constantly belittled by his contemporaries. Also his mind matured slowly, possibly from lack of vitality. Had he died in his fifties he would have had no great influence on world thought. At forty he did not know that he was going to be a philosopher, and at sixty-seven he was one of the greatest philosophers who ever lived.

Kant's early ambitions centered around his desire to be a college professor. Each time he applied for the position he was refused because of his most unprepossessing appearance. Mousy is the term by which he has been described. His one affectation was a manservant walking behind him holding an umbrella over his head.

When Kant was eighteen he decided that the secret of a high destiny was to decide what one intended to do, and then permit no force of circumstance to interfere with the accomplishment of that end. By consistently following that premise he finally achieved his professorship.

Kant was fifty-seven when he published his *Critique of Pure Reason*. The work resulted from years of slow and careful deductions. In this the power of reason is set up to limit the absolute free will of the individual by the ideas of duty and right. In the moral sphere virtue consists of obedience to the dictation of duty, which in turn is the constraint imposed by the legislative power of reason. Judgment is established as a middle ground between theoretical and practical knowledge. The power of judgment is to subordinate particulars to the universals from which they originate. The judgment operates partly by means of classification and partly by reflection.

What could be more Neoplatonic than Kant's suspension of particulars from their generals. Proclus more than a thousand years earlier referred to created things as effulgent blossoms suspended from their spiritual causes. Kant merely moved causation downward from the plane of pure consciousness to the plane of pure mentation.

Of the personal life of Immanuel Kant during his years of professorship at Konigsberg there is almost nothing to tell. The ordinary experiences that make up the life of the average person never touched this strange little man. According to one of his biographers his life passed like the most regular of regular verbs, but by the same definition it was an active verb with no passive form—but all the activity was internal.

In the years following the publication of *Critique of Pure Reason* Kant became an acknowledged leader in the intellectual world. Questions on every possible subject were brought to him, and his decisions were regarded as little less than scriptural. The philosopher enjoyed this high esteem with appropriate modesty, being too much involved in his own mental labors to appreciate the sphere of influence he had created. All went well until he extended his efforts into the province of theology. At that point he came into violent collision with the literal theological doctrine of the Lutheran Church. The chances are that he had little if any interest in the sectarianism of his day. He was looking for answers to questions, and his groping led him into the preserves of the Church.

We can imagine Kant wrestling with the problem of universal creation. If God created the world, who created God? What about evolution? Why must all life grow when an all-powerful God could have fashioned it perfect in the first place? If Deity is by nature all-powerful, all-wise, and all-good, why did it loose in space an infinite diversity of contradictions, discords, and contentions? How is the love of God to be reconciled with the obvious fact that all living things survive by destroying each other? Why must existence be an eternal struggle against adverse inevitables? What power in heaven or earth put into man's head the desire to be rich? Why is piety necessary; the process of being grateful for something we may never get? What is happiness, and how is it to be attained? Why did a perfect God fashion a human being so ignorant that he is incapable of understanding his own Father, and has to approach him by means of an involved, contradictory man-made theology? Why do we have disease, sin, and suffering? If these are in payment for some past evil action, why was that evil action necessary in the first place? Why does man make mistakes if he was fashioned in the image of his Creator? Does God make mistakes?

It was impossible to construct a philosophy without consideration of these vital issues, but it was inevitable that the reasoning power would come to conclusions contrary to Lutheranism. After Kant began his writings on *Religion within the Boundaries of Pure Reason,* the storm broke. Perhaps he believed his position was strong enough to risk the wrath of the clergy. If so he was presently disillusioned. The government forbade the little man any further pronouncements concerning the possible inconsistencies of Christian theology. He took refuge behind the strong walls of the University of Konigsberg, and with the permission of the faculty continued applying his *Critique* to the Lutheran dogma.

About that time Kant was accused of favoring the cause of the French Revolution, which the German princes were viewing with increasing alarm. The combination of the Lutheran clergy and the French Revolution influenced Frederick the Great of Prussia to forbid, on pain of the full weight of his imperial displeasure, any further excursions into the delicate subject of theology.

For the first time in his life Kant had to bow to a will stronger than his own. Although he seemed to accept the situation gracefully, his ego was mortally wounded. The interdict was lifted after the death of the king, but it was too late. The strong spirit had been broken by a single reverse, and never recovered its vigor. Kant's mind lacked the philosophic optimism and the depth of mystical understanding which could have carried him through his period of stress. Pure reason is of little comfort in adversity.

The little professor gave up most of his class work and withdrew more and more into himself. A corresponding decline attacked his mental vigor, and his last writings are a feeble restatement of his earlier works. Later he was afflicted with falling and fainting spells, and his sight was affected. Most of the symptoms indicate hypochondria and psychological frustration. Near the end of his life he broke one of his inflexible rules and permitted the services of a physician. He died on the 12th of February, 1804, having not quite completed his 80th year. He did not lose his mind, but he lost the power and intellectual brilliance of his earlier years.

Wordiness has been the peculiar burden of learning. Since the beginning of man's intellectual life he has involved his thoughts in abstruse terms under the delusion that obscurity of style was an indication of superiority of intellect. Charles Darwin managed to state the Darwinian theory in as many words as it was possible to bring to bear upon the subject. Herbert Spencer, a man of great idealism, was loquacious to the degree of exhaustion, and Huxley fell into a slough of words from which he never escaped. Even the fiction writers were afflicted with this malady of language. Dickens, Thackeray, and Scott, not to mention earlier novelists, were sincerely convinced that words were things to conjure with, and the magic they wrought was magnificent but enervating.

Immanuel Kant was a supreme master of the art of using words as a method of obscuring meanings. Will Durant in his *Story of Philosophy* thus footnotes his chapter on the immortal philosopher: "Kant himself is hardly intelligible, because his thought is insulated with a bizarre and intricate terminology (hence the paucity of direct quotation in this chapter)."

The Man Who Killed God

Kant's contemporaries ridiculed him for his obscurity of style. It was stated in his own time that in the process of his philosophy the little professor had killed God. It would be more accurate, it seems, to say that he murdered the meaning of words. Perhaps the dilemma is best expressed by an example. Here are a few simple lines of definition from the *Critique of Pure Reason*: "Thus Totality is nothing but Plurality contemplated as Unity; Limitation is merely Reality conjoined with Negation; Community is the Causality of a Substance, reciprocally determining, and determined by other substances; and finally Necessity is nothing but Existence, which is given through the Possibility itself."

The critical system of Kant is concerned with the study of the phenomena of consciousness in an effort to discover the invariable principles of knowledge, but even he could find no adequate definition for consciousness. He believed, however, that behind all manifestations of thought and action were invariable laws as exact as mathematics. To acquire knowledge is a duty, and to act in accordance with its principles is a virtue. He rescued mind from matter, and set up intellectual power as the ruler of personal life. But he immediately imposed strict rules upon the workings of the mind. These rules constitute the substance of reason, which must be the criterion of all values.

Seeking desperately for a peg of certainty on which to hang his system, Kant found mathematics the perfect and invariable science. He developed an almost fanatical devotion for the fact that three and three make six. Here was something simple, undeniable, and obvious. It never occurred to him that the very simplicity of this fact was the source of its strength and charm. Had he written his philosophy in words of one syllable his books would have had the weight of Scripture; as it is, he is studied mostly in digest form. Neither the university professor nor the thoughtful layman can enjoy their reading of Kant. The total lack of emotional content also detracts seriously from the readability of the texts.

Most persons looking for the reason behind the phenomena of life seek outwardly for the answers. Kant realized that the weakness of the sciences was due to the weakness of the scientist himself. There was nothing mysterious about life or living. Mysteries arose from misunderstanding. The mind which links the person desiring to know and the thing to be known was inadequate and subject to numerous fallacies.

When Kant picked up an apple his eyes told him it was an apple; when he smelled it his nose told him it was an apple; when he bit into it his sense of taste told him it was an apple; and when his fingers closed about it his sense of feeling told him that it was the shape of an apple. From all these testimonies he decided that he was holding an apple; this was highly reasonable. But suppose that the subject of his consideration was something (just as real as an apple) that his sensory perceptions could not agree upon, some of these senses perceiving it and others rejecting it. The result must be confusion. Man is a living, thinking, conscious creature connected with the universe about him only by means of his five senses—five little windows through which he must explore outer space. Unfortunately, the sense perceptions are peculiarly inept for the use that man wants to make of them.

The universe is not to blame for human suffering; it is man himself, who is incapable of seeing the large plan and

therefore unable to work in harmony with the purposes of
the world. This realization opened a large field of thought
for the professor. He had hit upon a great truth, which even
his mind could not fully comprehend.

After centuries of civilization and culture we still trust
implicitly in the testimonies revealed by the five little windows. And it seldom occurs to anyone to doubt the findings
of his senses. Kant asked the question, "Although all the
sense perceptions tell us that the object we are holding is an
apple, how do we know it to be a fact?" All that passes into
the mind from outside is merely testimony that it is an apple.
It is not even a picture of the apple. It is not something
round that the nerve impulses actually carry to the brain,
nor is it the taste of the apple; it is in truth only a series of
impulses bearing witness.

What makes an apple? Kant thought about that depress-
ing problem on many of his afternoon walks. What enables
man through his sensory perceptions to take one substance
and assert, "This is an apple." It never occurs to the average
individual who says, "This is a chair", to wonder how he
knows it is a chair. An actual chair does not go into the
brain; a series of impulses cannot of themselves have any
actual shape. Brought together, however, they are capable of
creating an internal pattern which we know to be a chair.
We look at people, but it is not our brain that sees their faces;
all that is received is a series of impulses. As these impulses
strike the brain they instantly create a pattern, and it is only
in this way that we see faces. Everything we do depends
upon the coming of these messages, and upon something
inside taking hold of these messages and making sense out
of them.

We always overlook the obvious. It required someone like Immanuel Kant to discover the marvelous machinery which enables us to see a teacup. The answer could not come to one who runs, so he walked slowly. He was resolved to discover what power there was in man which enabled him to say with assurance, "I see a teacup."

Out of his deliberations Kant divided life into two parts, the noumenal and the phenomenal existence. The noumenal, the causal factor, is inside of man and is the estimator and the weigher. The phenomenal is the thing outside of man which must be estimated and weighed. Phenomenal impulses are constantly going into the noumenal world; and equally constantly the noumenal is sending out reflexes and reactions. That seems rather simple, but it is not so obvious when Kant tells it in three hundred pages.

We are now presented with a number of important problems. We are made the victims of our own sensory perceptions. When the eyes fail we become blind; a part of the world is cut off from us. To the degree that the sensory perceptions are developed the impulses are correct, but even if all five senses are developed and bear testimony we have not seen all; intangible things must still be considered. Intangibles remain mysterious, not because they are real mysteries but because we have no way of estimating them. It is this line of thought which caused Kant to be included among the transcendentalists.

The universe is mathematical—absolute order and absolute consistency. Two important things about the universe we can grasp in part. One is time and the other is place. Time is a pet illusion of some schools and a pet reality of others. Time creates the possibility of a sequence. Time is the measure of the order of circumstances and incidents. For instance, the Old Testament in the original Hebrew form was written without tense. That has left us very uncertain about biblical chronology. With the time factor missing we do not know when things happened, and the sequence of cause and effect is broken. If we do not know the relation of one incident to another we cannot draw any moral conclusions from the order of happenings. Time as we know it is swallowed up in eternity, and is only a device of man. Yet whether it is a device of man or a reality, it is necessary as one of the factors in estimating life.

Place is the other important element. What is located in time and place is capable of definition. If it is not in time or in place it is not capable of definition. Hence it is impossible to define God, whose time and place boundaries are unknowable.

The Critique of Pure Reason

Kant's mind was constantly developed to the establishment of certain boundaries in the universal mystery. These boundaries were law and order, time and place, sequence and circumstance, and in his *Critique of Pure Reason,* which is not really a critical work, we are given the fruits of his research.

No great system of philosophy merely tells someone that he is wrong; it attempts to point out the proper means for solution. Kant is very sincere in his effort to point out the correct course of action, both in the accumulation of facts and the assimilation of knowledge. Philosophy can be defined as a pattern for reasonable living. He accepted this viewpoint and offered these suggestions: You are a part of the universe; you exist in time and place; you are a fragment existing within a larger fragment. Therefore, if you wish to exist toward survival you must play the game of life according to the laws of the larger fragment, which is your world. Right and wrong are agreement with or departure from the morals and ethics of the larger universe. If you agree with the pattern of the world you are right. If you disagree with the pattern of the world you are wrong, and will be punished by the simple circumstance of maladjustment.

So Kant, like the Taoists of China, advised the individual to pattern his conduct after universals rather than according to the dictates of men.

Buried in the curious phraseology of his writings Kant introduced the term *categorical imperative* for a moral law that is unconditional or absolute, or whose validity or claim does not depend on any ulterior motive or end. If you wish to live well you must so conduct yourself that if your way of life were applied to all creatures there would be no injustice in the universe. This was the little professor's substitute for the Golden Rule. For example, some men want to accumulate worldly goods. If every creature in the universe desired to accumulate, could each have sufficient for its needs?

Consider theology, a most vexing issue. Is it conceivable that the great suns moving in space and the tiny electrons moving an atom are arguing about their religious denomination? Furthermore, would they be any wiser, better, or happier if they devoted themselves to such a pursuit? If not, there is no likelihood of such arguments proving profitable to the human being.

Suppose you have a tendency to lose your temper under certain provocation. How does this fit into the order of the world? If God lost his temper and sulked in space, what would happen to mortal creation? Research indicates that God has an even disposition, and if you would be godlike the divine example is worth following.

It was no intention of Kant to remove the Creator from his universe. He tried rather to prove that the world was ruled by a principle and not by a person; by laws rather than by whims; by reason rather than by despotism. Out of a misunderstanding of his philosophy has come modern materialism. Kant did not intend to kill God but to destroy a false conception of God which had originated in ignorance of the universal plan. We now realize that he was right when he impersonalized Deity and recognized God as the reality behind the world manifesting through law and made visible through form. The universe is the embodiment of principles, and God who is the father of all is not a fretful old man who hardened Pharaoh's heart, but an immutable principle manifesting as wisdom, virtue, strength, and beauty.

The writings of Kant present a marked contrast to those of the philosophers who preceded him, for example Sir Francis Bacon and René Descartes. Bacon, though also a small man physically, was a philosophical optimist, and idealist. His philosophy was based upon a broad Platonic tolerance of thinking; it was great, gentle, and noble. The Platonic philosophy invites us to see the good in everything, and inclines us to forgive the faults and limitations of our fellow creatures. Most of all it preserves Deity as a moral entity. God indeed is in his heaven and all is right with the world.

In the Academy at Athens it was Aristotle who sat to one side listening and doubting. Broad generalizations were not enough on which to build a philosophy of particulars. If certain general facts were true, it must be possible to prove them, at least dialectically. So Aristotle set up the machinery of categories to put the world in order, and this heritage of mental tidiness was passed on to Immanuel Kant, the person-ification of neatness and precision. To Kant there must be certain categories of knowledge; whether they are pessimistic or optimistic, whether idealistic or materialistic, they must be accepted because they are necessary. He demanded absolute philosophical integrity. Perhaps honesty was sometimes brutal and unpleasant, but it was man's duty to face the facts. In this he differed from Plato, who might have defined honesty as a gentle acceptance of the beauty and goodness everywhere present in the world.

The little professor of Konigsberg was not by nature bel-ligerent or intentionally dictatorial; he was shy, reticent, and kindhearted. He had a particular affection for young people, and was always ready to guide them with sound and practical advice. He preferred to recognize the better side of human nature, and held few grudges. He was as generous as meager means would allow, but never permitted students to attend his classes without payment of the prescribed fee. This was a matter of principle, for he sincerely believed that it weak-ened character to ease the path of learning. Those who struggle for what they want gain the strength to use that which they learn.

The Dignity of Duty

Kant had great regard for what he called duty. To be morally worth while, an action must be inspired by a sense of responsibility. Here again he is obscure, for it is not exactly plain what he meant by the word duty, or the degree of emotional content present in the concept of responsibility. But not given to glamorizing his doctrine, he probably meant the rather tedious implications we now associate with the thought.

The merit of action is gained not by the consequences achieved but from the integrity of the motive. It may be that we cannot accomplish the end which duty dictates, but if we try we establish moral worth, and this increases with the prolonged consistency of effort. The greater the obstacles which stand between us and the fulfillment of our moral action, the greater the merit stored up within us.

It is our primary duty to live according to our conception of life. When we discover the laws governing the universal plan we are responsible to ourselves for a way of conduct in harmony with those laws. The highest moral virtue is, therefore, obedience to the dictates of conviction. Conversely, moral delinquency is to believe one thing and practice its contrary. Courage is the power to be true to ourselves.

Kant did not consider the possibility that a sense of duty could result in a variety of oppressive devotions. Some of the most unhappy and destructive actions which mortals have indulged in were inspired by a perverted sense of duty. To be true to self, the self must be true to truth. This comes back to Pilate's question which Jesus did not answer, "What is truth?"

It is inconceivable that man can attain perfect understanding by the reasoning powers alone. The emotions also must play their part in the ennobling of human character. The emotions always play havoc with rational systems of thought.

Intuition is closely associated with the sublimation of the emotional content in the human personality. By intuition an inspirational power is released by which man is brought into direct contact with universal values. Kant could not know this because it was beyond his experience.

Kant would not accept the miraculous as a means of proving a religious tradition. In the first place, it is difficult to secure an accurate description of an extraphysical phenomenon. Under the glamour of the incident the mind is lured away from a critical analysis and falls into self-deception. In the second place, our comparative ignorance of the laws governing matter and mind makes it impossible for us to fit the apparently unreasonable incident into the larger pattern of universal reasonableness.

Kant also discounted prayer on the ground that to pray for that which is contrary to the law of life is to demand the impossible. A law which can be deflected by the supplications of fretful and selfish mortals would be of little use in maintaining the harmony of the world. He saved his bitterest denunciations, however, for those theological institutions which aligned themselves with political despotism, using their religious influence as a means for perpetuating intellectual and physical tyranny. It was at this stage of his philosophy that he came into conflict with Lutheran Protestantism.

The practical application of Kant's philosophy comes with the realization that the human mind possesses the power to resist the pressure of circumstances. It can accept or reject the sensations which flow into it from environment, tradition, and experimentation. Man is not a mere victim of his world; he makes or unmakes his own destiny, and can be wiser than his time through self-discipline. Good and evil are not facts in themselves; they are interpretations set up within the individual. We are not destined to misery because those about us are devoted to perverted codes of living. Each of us can live well anywhere, anytime, if we know how to live in obedience to universal law.

It was inevitable that so revolutionary a viewpoint would produce numerous and distinguished adversaries. The confusion was increased by the obscurity of Kant's style, which opened his writings to a variety of misunderstandings. The principal objections were that the Kantian system destroyed all rational belief in God, undermined man's conviction of the immortality of the soul, and negated the objective reality of knowledge. If we cannot trust our intuitions in matters mystical and theological, and cannot trust the testimony of our sense perceptions in matters physical and material, wherein shall we rest our faith?

Among the important philosophers to be influenced by Kant's critical method are Johann Gottlieb Fichte and Friedrich Wilhelm Joseph von Schelling. Both of these men established permanent places for themselves in the sphere of dialectic knowledge. Schelling, in an effort to amend Kant's system, made use of his profound acquaintance with the theories of Plato, Bruno, and Spinoza. He defined virtue as "a state of the soul in which it conforms itself not to an external law but an internal necessity of its own nature." He further defined history as the progressively developed revelation of Deity. Here we see God returning to his original place as the source of all good and the end of all philosophy.

In Schelling's system, the infinite life at the source of all things attains self-development according to three motions or movements. The first is reflection, by which the Infinite embodies itself in the finite. The second is subsumption, by which the absolute liberates itself from the finite state. The third movement is reason, which is a neutral ground wherein the two former movements are blended and balanced. After Schelling came the chaos, and the German school of philosophy specialized itself into a number of systems with only mutual antagonism in common.

"The end of philosophy," wrote Plato, "is the intuition of unity." Yet the moment we attempt to examine the phenomena of life we are inclined to depart from unity and set up difference as a means of comparison and estimation. Perception is an action which involves unification. It is the reflection upon the things perceived that immediately tends toward analysis. According to Anaxagoras, "The mind knows only when it subdues its objects; when it reduces the many to the one."

Both Leibnitz and Kant attempted to reveal the nature of true knowledge as multitude in unity. Division exists within fact, but fact itself is never divided. We have the privilege of examining diversity as far as the intellect will permit and at the same time retain the realization of its basic oneness. The moment we lose sight of unity we are outside the bounds of reason. Pythagoras used numbers to reveal the mystery of unity. One is the perfect number because it is the unit and the unity, the one and the all. Within the nature of the one exists the other numerals. Two, for example, is not two ones, but one in the term of halves. Three is one in the term of thirds, and so on. This is a subtle point, but it is the sure foundation of knowledge. The only possible way of escaping dualism is to recognize it as a division within unity and not a division of unity.

Kant was particularly weak in his estimation of aesthetics, and we may infer that he was little given to artistic emotions. To him art was a production. Mechanical art was the performance of a certain prescribed technique for the attainment of a definite purpose. Aesthetic art had pleasure as its immediate purpose, and fine art implied that pleasure was under the criticism of judgment.

The problem of beauty caused the little professor considerable difficulty. He finally decided that in quality beauty is that which pleases without any particular interest in the object itself. In quantity, beauty implies a universal pleasure because we expect others to share our enjoyment. In relation, beauty is a form without any particular end because we do not expect utility as an attribute of pleasure. In modality, beauty is a necessary satisfaction; that which is truly beautiful must cause pleasure. Kant tried a little harder with this problem, and concluded that the agreeable stimulates desire, the good gives motive to the will, and the beautiful demands the reaction of pleasure.

In all this ponderous effort to rationalize aesthetic impulse Kant was handicapped by the fact that, so far as history records, he never personally experienced a spontaneous emotion. We can compare his definitions with the simple nobility of Neoplatonic mysticism. Plotinus in his essay *On The Beautiful* tells us simply that beauty is the will of God revealed in the patterns of nature. Wherever there is law working without opposition the patterns that are set up reveal the unity of life, the ever-present good, and the power of the soul over form. We call this revelation beauty.

Most of the philosophers we have written of in these books were men who lived rich and diversified lives. They mingled with every type of mind, and according to the opportunities of their time were widely traveled. Most of them accepted the challenge of personal problems, and from depth of experience and breadth of vision evolved their systems. Kant never traveled. He built an impervious wall between himself and personal living. Confusion interfered with the continuity of his thinking. All interruptions were disagreeable to him. He read considerably, but did not find books open doors to intellectual adventure. He was impressed principally by the stupidity of the authors because they failed in what he considered a proper measure of intellectual criticism.

Philosophy is a way of life, and it is impossible to perfect the structure of inner conviction without actual experience. Whenever Kant touched on a living issue he retired behind his wall of theories. He was profound but not well-balanced, and his system suffered from a lack in the man himself. Kant was so depressed by the sight of suffering that he refused to visit a sick friend. When Plato was informed that a student or acquaintance was ill he hastened to him immediately that he might bring consolation and wisdom. Saint Augustine on his deathbed received a supplicant who sought comfort. These incidents alone reveal the difference between classical idealism and modern rationalism.

The results of Kant's teachings have been incalculable. It is safe to say that all philosophy after his time was influenced by his method. While this is especially true of German philosophy, it is also generally true of most other European and American schools. After revising, amending, reforming, and recriticizing Kant, we have as a final product mechanism, the pride of the modern intellectual. Mechanistic materialism may be defined as the total eclipse of idealism in formal thinking. The universe is a machine, self-creating, self-operating, and capable of repairing itself if it breaks down. There is no need for God or any spiritual cause behind the phenomena of the world. This smug, practical, and completely intellectual solution to the larger problems of living and thinking now dominates the sphere of higher education.

Skepticism approaching cynicism is a sophisticated and superficial attitude, and of little help in time of trouble. It flourishes in eras of prosperity when the human being is very sure of himself and filled with conceits about the magnitude of his own accomplishments. Conversely, it languishes whenever mankind gets into serious trouble. The successful business man adding up his profits in the security of his sumptuously appointed offices talks glibly about his materialistic convictions. It is part of the philosophy of rugged individualism and the survival of the fittest. But when tragedy strikes, when depressions sweep away financial security, and when wars threaten the life and happiness of the individual, mechanistic materialism loses general favor. When we do not need God we are materialists, but when we are in trouble we become idealists.

Kant did not intend that his philosophy should breed an utter materialism. It was his desire merely to clarify the position of the human mind in relationship to the phenomena of the outer world. But he supplied the instruments necessary to the fashioning of a broad skepticism. The disciples of Kant outdid their master in zeal if not in judgment, using his means to justify their own ends.

A Priori and A Posteriori

There are two terms in philosophy which we should all understand, *a priori* and *a posteriori*. Kant defines a priori knowledge as that which exists absolutely independent of experience, and a posteriori knowledge as that which can be derived only from experience. By acknowledging the existence of a priori knowledge, Kant deserves to be included among the Platonists. Knowledge can arise from within the individual and manifest in the form of unalterable convictions, that relate to the existence of God, the reality of Good, and the immortality of the human soul. None of these convictions arise directly from experience, but may receive certain justification or proof from experience.

A priori knowledge is concerned for the most part with subjects beyond analysis by the reason. They arise from an internal necessity, and are justified by that necessity.

A posteriori knowledge has its origin in individual or common experience. By larger implication it becomes the basis of all sciences which originate in the observation of phenomena and its classification into categories. Materialism is built upon the foundation of a posteriori knowledge, and theoretically at least its doctrines are provable by experience. A laboratory, for example, is a place set aside for the intensification of experience along specialized lines. It sometimes happens that experience comes into conflict with internal conviction, and this is responsible for the disunity in the fields of learning.

Plato has come to be recognized as the personification of a priori knowledge and Aristotle the personification of a posteriori knowledge. These two men are the embodiments of the eternal conflict between the internal and the external for dominion over the intellect. Plato has been favored by the laity because he personifies the hopes of man and the human dream toward universal good. Aristotle is admired by the trained thinker because his conclusions are based upon facts which can be experienced by the intellect.

Mysticism, which was the Neoplatonic contribution, sought to bind up the wounds caused by the extremists of the two previous groups. The Neoplatonists taught that it was possible to experience a priori knowledge. Man, by perfecting the internal extrasensory perceptions, could explore cause with the same security with which he now examines only effects.

All of the great philosophers have contributed something to the enrichment of the rational tradition. Even materialism will in the end play its part in the perfection of human ideals. By exploring every possible aspect of the world as thought and experience we are gradually but inevitably approaching the realization of unity. As the philosopher must experience all things himself in order to attain ultimate wisdom, so philosophical systems must examine every part of nature, human and divine, before the ultimate synthesis is possible. Through diversity we are becoming aware of unity. Through the many we are discovering the one. But when that discovery is complete we shall be aware of the dignity of the one because we have examined thoroughly all of its parts and members. We approached philosophy first as a study of the anatomy of the divine man; now we must go further and realize that the next step is to regard philosophy as the physiology of space.

RALPH WALDO EMERSON

7

THE NEW ENGLAND TRANSCENDENTALISTS

Ralph Waldo Emerson, the Sage of Concord

Eclecticism, the Poor-Man's Philosophy

THE charm and power of the philosophic way of life are revealed particularly through the diversity of temperaments which have dedicated themselves to the service of wisdom. There was gentle Plato and critical Aristotle, skeptical Socrates and cynical Diogenes, ecstatic Plotinus and repentant Augustine; each was different in the quality of his vision and the capacity to interpret that vision, yet all were devoted to the service of the human need. Such, then, is the power of philosophy that it can adapt any instrument to its eternal purposes.

Certainly it is easier to define philosophy than it is to describe philosophers. In the present work we have traced the lives and teachings of several great men. Here we have met pious Aquinas, bombastic Paracelsus, noble Bacon and humble Boehme, methodical Kant and friendly Emerson. Each was a distinct human being with a highly specialized type of mind, and there was little in common in their person-

191

alities and temperaments, yet they shared one disposition—
love of learning—which manifested as an irresistible impulse
to improve the spiritual state of their fellow creatures. Truth
was their journey, and they traveled far.

In presenting a survey of world thought covering a wide
vista of time and place it is pertinent to warn the reader
against the dangers of eclecticism. In simple definition eclecticism is a system of thinking which advocates the selection
of useful or acceptable doctrines from various sources without
consideration of the inconsistencies which may exist among
the basic principles involved. The eclectic method has been
called the poor man's philosophy for the reason that the
majority of untrained thinkers fall into the basic dilemma
which it presents.

Eclecticism provides a Roman holiday for the skeptics,
and these doubting Thomases are forever pointing out the irreconcilable differences between systems of thinking to the
end of proving the universal absence of truth. How can we
be sure of anything, they ask, in the presence of a general
and ably-sustained disagreement?

Syncretism takes the attitude of compromise, recommend-
ing a broad modification of all extreme doctrines in the cause
of consistency. Therefore it may be defined as the philosophy of appeasement. But the eclectic is not burdened with
any reasonable or unreasonable doubts. If he comes upon an
idea which is satisfactory to his needs and purposes he in-
corporates it into the body of his doctrine, whether it be
Eastern or Western, ancient or modern, orthodox or unorthodox.

The ancient Romans were by temperament and circumstance given to eclecticism, and outstanding among them in
this persuasion were Cicero, Marcus Aurelius and Boethius.

In the opinion of Edward Gibbon, Boethius was the last
Roman whom Cato or Tully could have acknowledged for
a countryman. With him the structure of pagan idealism
came to an end.

That great and noble thoughts are to be found in all systems of philosophy is undeniable, and the liberality of mind
which realizes and accepts this fact certainly is commendable.
But the danger lies in the tendency to accept a variety of ideas
without sufficient thoughtfulness. A philosophic school is a
systematic development of basic principles applied to a variety
of intellectual particulars. In all systematic procedure the
conclusion is suspended from logical premises, and in turn
becomes an element in further compounds. Separated from
the system of which it is a part, the fragment loses its vitality
and is no longer useful as an instrument of judgment.

There is an interesting fable which illustrates this situation.
The truth seeker is represented as a kindly and well-disposed
man wandering along a country lane bordered with countless
wild flowers, their beautiful blossoms symbolizing noble
thoughts. The wanderer is inspired to gather a bouquet of
many colors to ornament his house, and does not realize that
the moment he picks the blossoms from their parent stem
they will die. The beauty will linger for a short time, but
the flowers must fade because the source of their life is gone.

Eclecticism, like a nosegay of bright flowers, pleases the
eye, satisfies the emotion, and ornaments the person; it is the
philosophy of the dilettante, pleasing but perishable. Because
all of the colors of nature are harmonious the flowers look
well together, but each has an integrity of its own which is
lost by those who admire only the general effect. It does not
follow that we should close our minds to the good thoughts
of other men, and it is here that Neoplatonism points the way

to solution. Like Buddhism in Asia, this Alexandrian school extended its influence through a diversity of sects and creeds without falling into the eclectical error. First the individual must establish his philosophy of life—a large general framework of invariable universal laws. Into this inclusive generality he may then incorporate any number of diverse particulars by subjecting them to the censorship of trained reason. We can be eclectic only to the degree that our intellect can fit a variety of details into a well-developed reference frame. We may accept as many ideas as we can unify by the strength of our own understanding. All difference is circumscribed by unity, even as all nature with its infinite variety of manifestations is within one principle of being. Whoever discovers the one can safely consider the phenomena of the many, but if the one is not clearly known by inner experience the pageantry of the many presents a hopeless confusion.

All men are profoundly influenced by the styles and habits of their times. It is natural for democratic systems of government to foster eclectic systems of thinking. We mistake lack of thoroughness for liberality of mind. Intellectual tolerance infers the right of each individual to express his own convictions, but it does not necessarily follow that each must embrace the convictions of other men in order to convey the impression of broad-mindedness. The breadth of modern experience confronts each of us with a diversity of human ideas, and the temptation to believe everything is as dangerous as the temptation to believe nothing. Possibly the ancient world was stronger and more consistent in its intellectual processes because the area of its practical experience was more restricted. We are greatly influenced by the thoughts of those about us, and this pressure overwhelms the integrity of our own intellect. We agree with all because it is the easier way.

Having committed ourselves it becomes a duty to defend our commitments, and thinking degenerates into intellectual ingenuity. We are broad-minded simply because it is the fashion of our time, but we are not thorough for the reason that systematic thinking is not a part of our experience.

It is usual for writers dealing with the subject of American philosophy to divide our systems into two broad classifications—imported and indigenous. Up to the present time most of our intellectual tradition has come from Europe. This is as true of art, literature, science, and religion, as it is of philosophy. To date, the most noticeable break away from foreign influence has been in architecture, which is taking on a strong indigenous quality. In recent years there has been a considerable influx of orientalism, but as yet this has not made any deep impression upon our academic structure.

In many respects Ralph Waldo Emerson personified the finer qualities of our American way of thinking, which is an extension of Roman intellectualism. He was certainly an eclectic, deriving his inspiration from a variety of comparatively unrelated sources. In his personality was that delicate balance of aristocracy and democracy which is an outstanding feature of our culture. Everything that he taught was idealistic, liberal, and humanitarian, but the man himself was as conservative as any Brahman, genteel in the extreme, and completely aloof from the humanity which he loved and served. He had a profound regard for mankind as a whole, but was not especially patient or tolerant of any man in particular.

New England Romanticism

Emerson was the central figure in a group of philosophically inclined men and women who have come to be known as the New England Transcendentalists. The group included a number of our most brilliant intellectuals. Immanuel Kant used the word transcendental to signify that which transcended or went beyond the experience, especially the capacity of the mind to achieve a true state of knowledge. Later the word took on an extremely vague connotation, and was applied to a variety of mystical and metaphysical cults. With Emerson transcendentalism was an extreme intuitionalism growing out of the increasing influence of the Unitarian movement. Emphasis was placed upon the internal capacity of the individual to solve the problems of his life by the private practice of a broad and liberal idealism.

The outstanding exponents of this New England romanticism, in addition to Emerson, were Nathaniel Hawthorne, Henry Wadsworth Longfellow, John Greenleaf Whittier, Oliver Wendell Holmes, James Russell Lowell, and Henry David Thoreau. The writings of Thoreau in particular influenced the career of the prominent Hindu idealist and social reformer, Mohandas Gandhi.

Perhaps we cannot do better than to define New England transcendentalism in Emerson's own words: "Man has a body, wherein he is allied to the beasts; reason, which is his peculiar endowment; a soul, which connects him with Deity. As an animal, he has instincts, love for food, pleasure, which we term appetites; as rational man, love for truth, intuitions of the understanding, sympathies as a member of the human family, affections of the heart; as a child of God, religious aspirations. He is not merely an animal; nor an animal with reason. His nature is triple—animal, rational, spiritual; and it is to those systems, on whatever subject, which contemplate him as a spiritual being, that we apply the term transcendental.

That belief we term Transcendentalism which maintains that man has ideas, that come not through the five senses, or the powers of reasoning; but are either the result of direct revelation from God, his immediate inspiration, or his immanent presence in the spiritual world." *Transcendentalism and Other Addresses.*

It does not require deep learning to discover the source of this Emersonian definition. The words are rich with the gentle nobility of Pythagoras, Plato, and Plotinus. Emerson was widely read in the classical philosophy of the Greeks, and was strongly persuaded by the utopian dream which dominated the inspiration of the Greek idealists. His first essay, written while he was a student at Harvard, was entitled *The Character of Socrates.* His opinion of Plato may be estimated from a few brief quotations. In one place he writes, "Out of Plato come all things that are still written and debated among men of thought." Later he adds, "Plato is philosophy, and philosophy, Plato..." In the same essay he tells us, "... the writings of Plato have preoccupied every school of learning, every lover of thought, every church, every poet—making it impossible to think, on certain levels, except through him. He stands between the truth and every man's mind, and has almost impressed language and the primary forms of thought with his name and seal." Emerson referred to the Alexandrian Neoplatonists as "a constellation of genius."

It is not too much to say that the New England Transcendentalists were in fact Platonists and Neoplatonists, and one cannot contemplate the deep and patient idealism of these American scholars without feeling very close to the classical nobility of the old Academy. Platonism was built upon the recognition of the threefold constitution of man. First there is the body which is the proper receptacle for the superior principle, but is itself an animal nature. Second there is the intellect, the power of self-knowing, that extension of the mind into the sphere of reason by which it is possible for the human being to become a philosopher. And third there is that spiritual and divine part eternally verging toward God and seeking to attain that mystical union with Deity which is the end of all growth and aspiration. These are the Platonic principles restated in Emerson's definition of transcendentalism.

This strange mystical way of thought could not have stemmed from the Platonic method unless Neoplatonism had emphasized the mystical theology of Plato. The New England intellectuals were Neoplatonic mystics rather than Platonic philosophers. Of course this restriction of definition is made in deference to modern methods of classification. It assumes the possibility of separating one stream of tradition into two degrees or aspects, one essentially intellectual and the other essentially spiritual. How many of those who have loved the poems and essays of Emerson realize that through him they have touched the fringe of Plato's robe?

Durant in his *Story of Philosophy* gives only four short quotations from Emerson, and does not include him in his group of outstanding thinkers. Emerson belonged to a school of thought that is not generally admired by the scholars of today. Like the music and art of his time, his philosophy is not regarded today as virile or dynamic; it is not filled with criticisms, nor does it survive by attacking the opinions of other systems. The ideals of transcendentalism are not to be found in our American philosophers William James and John Dewey, nor in our adopted son George Santayana.

These ideals belonged to a race of thinkers that is rapidly disappearing.

The world in which Emerson lived had little in common with this amazing generation with its intense competitive industrialism, so he has come to be regarded as old-fashioned, lacking the brittle brilliance which we demand from current intellectuals. Not the founder of any great doctrine, Emerson has been the inspiration of uncounted thousands who have loved the clarity of his words and the deep humanness of this dear old eclectic.

In his essay *Plato; or, The Philosopher* Emerson observed that "Great geniuses have the shortest biographies. Their cousins can tell you nothing about them." The intellectual activities of thoughtful persons do not make exciting reading. The man lives in his works and these works are the story of the man. All writings are to a degree autobiographical. Some live adventurous lives exploring strange countries in distant regions; others live adventurous thoughts, journeying far in the fourth dimensional vistas of mental space. Emerson was an armchair adventurer. Sitting quietly under the friendly shade of Concord's stately elms he sent forth his spirit along the old road that leads to the philosophic empire.

Emerson, the Unitarian

Ralph Waldo Emerson, American poet, essayist, and philosopher, was born in Boston, Massachusetts, on the 25th of May, 1803. His background was strongly religious, and at least seven of his ancestors were New England clergymen. It was quite natural, therefore, that the religious content in his nature should develop early and dominate his interests.

The Emerson family appears to have been extremely pur-itanical in its convictions. Puritanism was a by-product of the Protestant Reformation. It was religion deprived of most of its emotional content, and those who practiced its tenets developed a peculiar intensity, which invariably results from the frustration of the aesthetic impulses. Life among the New England Puritans was a serious business. Traditions were strong, and there was constant emphasis upon the cultiva-tion and practice of the homely virtues. Even in later life Emerson reflected much of the conservative atmosphere in which he was reared. This curious conflict between inherited conservativeness and acquired liberalism is reflected in many of his opinions. His viewpoint on woman's suffrage is typical of his divided allegiances. He was definitely in favor of women having social, educational, and political equality with men, but was markedly distressed at the thought of the various public gatherings in which these principles were agitated. Women in politics was a good idea, but women politicians were not an attractive lot according to the Emersonian criteria.

At one time in his life our philosopher was intrigued by the notion that a well-balanced personality should include a certain amount of time devoted to manual labor, so he took a hoe and went out into his garden each day in the hope of cultivating a fondness for agrarian pursuits. After a time he noticed that strenuous physical exercise interfered seriously with his intellectual activities. He was too tired to write well after this unaccustomed exercise, and in the end forsook the idea as impractical.

In the same vein Emerson decided that democracy should be applied to the servant question. He had two servants, and resolved that they should eat at the family table on the basis of entire equality. In this instance it was the hired help who rebelled, insisting that it greatly increased their work and made it impossible for them to prepare and serve the food properly. They appreciated the sentiment, but preferred to run the kitchen according to the traditional plan.

When Emerson was only eight years old his father, who was the minister of the First Unitarian Church of Boston, died suddenly, leaving his eight children without adequate financial protection, a condition not uncommon among the clergy. Young Ralph then came under the influence of a spinster aunt, Mary Moody Emerson, whom historians have liked to term eccentric. But if her attitudes were conventional and her mental horizons limited, her ambitions for the young nephew were sincere. She recognized the signs of genius and did everything possible to further his career. It was the lady's fond hope that Ralph would become a distinguished clergy-man and outshine all the other ministers who had ornamented the family tree. Miss Mary was a lonely, introverted soul, blighted by the pressure of New England puritanism. The tragedy of her own life impelled her toward the consolation of religion, but as surely as she pressed her faith upon her nephew so surely he drew away, not violently but quietly and firmly. Her beliefs could not be his. He was born with a breadth of mind that rebelled against all formal limitations upon thought and action.

Emerson entered Harvard College in 1817, and the records indicate that he was an average student. By no stretch of the imagination could he be regarded as an infant prodigy. He showed greatest aptitude for literature, but most of his college essays were exceedingly dull. His early love of poetry was not regarded as a valuable asset, but his ability at public speak-ing would be useful if he decided upon the ministry as a career. At that period his reading, though extensive, was en-

tirely proper and conventional. He promised to be an
eminently satisfactory member of an intensely smug orthodox
community.

Ralph's brother, William Emerson, was the head of a
school for refined young ladies in Boston. After graduating
from Harvard Ralph accepted an appointment to teach in
this school. He endured the superficial atmosphere of these
genteel and decadent surroundings for three years, and then,
urged on by Aunt Mary, decided to strike out for himself,
seeking a life work which would reflect his own individual
taste and growing abilities.

The natural outlet was the ministry, and young Emerson
decided that he had heard the call of the spirit. He became
a minister in 1826 and carried on the duties for a time with
considerable success. It was inevitable, however, that his
broad philosophic views should come into conflict with orthodox belief. He finally resigned his position as minister
of the Second Unitarian Church of Boston. Poor health
may have hastened his decision, as he was threatened with
tuberculosis. He preached occasionally from various pulpits
for a number of years, and throughout his life retained much
of the stamp of a dignified clergyman.

During the earlier years of his life Emerson's contact with
the larger world of the mind was principally through reading.
He became seriously interested in the writings of Emanuel
Swedenborg, the Swedish seer, but it does not appear that he
ever immersed himself in spiritism or psychical phenomena.
The essays of Carlyle were especially stimulating and satisfy-
ing. Later a lifetime friendship developed between these two
men.

In 1833 Emerson went to Europe, visited the places associated with his reading, and made personal contacts with

Coleridge, Wordsworth, and Carlyle. There can be no doubt that his visit to the shrines of European intellectualism broadened his vision and deepened his understanding. He became a citizen of the world with a perspective impossible to those content to remain at home.

Returning from his European wanderings Emerson lived with his mother in the old family home in Concord, and set about establishing himself in the lecture field. He was a born speaker, and success came to him almost immediately. In fact, lecturing was his profession, and the essays for which he is now best loved and remembered were compiled from the notes of various talks which he gave through the years. Although carefully prepared, his lectures had an inspirational quality which deeply influenced the thought of his time. He spoke with the quiet dignity of a religious man, and with a quaintness of style which fascinated his listeners.

In the fall of 1835 Emerson married Lydia Jackson of Plymouth. He took his bride to Concord and established her in one of those comfortable old houses which contribute to the charm of New England. Here with a fine garden, a charming wife, and the two previously mentioned domestics, he settled down to the calm, placid life of a small town squire. He took a constructive part in the life of the community, and was by nature sufficiently prudent and conservative to win the respect and confidence of his neighbors and fellow townsmen. Their feelings are evidenced by a number of anecdotes. For example, when the Emerson house burned down the community rebuilt it for him by popular subscription.

Caution is a philosophic virtue, and it is quite possible that the citizens of Concord would have viewed Emerson in a different light had they known the full measure of his thought. His interest in Hinduism, for example, would certainly have sent a ripple of consternation through the community, but he was wise enough to teach Hindu philosophy without reference to its origin or its terms. In fact, he was able to make it sound quite Unitarian, and everyone was content.

Emerson made a second visit to England in 1847 and gave a number of lectures, but the busy world was not for him. He detested crowds, confusion, and congestion. Hotels wearied his soul, and public applause was no panacea for these ailments. Quiet Concord was his world. There he could be with friends of his own selection, at peace with himself and at peace with the world. He was not snobbish, but aloof, preferring solitude and his own thoughts.

There is little to tell about the long, calm years of Emerson's life. He met every responsibility with Puritan thoroughness, and there lurked about him a shy sense of humor which added greatly to the charm of his person and mitigated the ills that flesh must bear.

When Emerson was sixty-three Harvard College bestowed upon him the degree of LL.D. The philosopher accepted this token of esteem with befitting modesty. Worldly honors are of little importance to a man whose physical life have reached its declining years. It is the habit of great institutions to honor ability too late. Recognition that might have eased earlier years of struggle is withheld until the struggle and the need are past.

In 1872 Emerson made a third visit to the old world. This time he went as far as Egypt, visiting the monuments of an old civilization that had always been close to his heart. Such a trip was arduous for a man of his years, and after his return there was a noticeable decrease of his intellectual vigor.

Emerson died on the 27th of April, 1882. Although his
mental powers had been waning for some years, he remained
to the end a quiet, cheerful man, one of a sturdy stock whose
convictions were deep and strong against the vicissitudes of
fortune. He was buried in the quaint old cemetery of Sleepy
Hollow among the traditions which he loved so well. His
home has become a shrine, and his library shelves are still
laden with the books he loved. I examined his library a short
time ago and found it packed with solid philosophic scholarship. In many of the books are neat notes and observations.
These should be collected and published, for they give a
wealth of insight into the character of the man and the quality
of his thinking.

Emerson's place in the world of philosophy is quite different from that of the others whose teachings we have
considered. He was an interpreter rather than an originator,
choosing to dedicate his life to the dissemination of the good
which came out of the minds of the past. Although he formulated no system he fashioned from the thoughts of other
men a viewpoint peculiarly his own. He felt no compulsion,
like that which motivated Kant, to integrate a universal
scheme. Nor was he like Boehme, a man of visions and mystical experiences. Cast in a Unitarian mold yet unable to
subscribe to the limitations imposed by denominationalism, he
may be defined as an inclusive Christian thinker. We say
inclusive because he was able to rejoice in the beauty and
purity of the world-mind as it manifested through the religions and philosophies of all nations and of all times. To
him a universal appreciation of good was Unitarianism. He
could accept no lower standard as appropriate to the Christian
life.

Emerson's Christianity can be best described by a quotation from the Christian Platonic philosopher St. Augustine: "That which is called the Christian Religion existed among the Ancients, and never did not exist, [sic] from the beginning of the human race until Christ came in the flesh, at which time the true religion which already existed began to be called Christianity."

Motivated by his realization that truth is everywhere present in nature, the Sage of Concord accepted the challenge of this larger vision and dedicated his intellectual resources to the simple restatement of the Neoplatonic doctrine of mystical participation. Modern academic philosophers approach Emersonianism with the same mental reservations with which they regard the Alexandrian mystics. The intellectualist is uncomfortable in the presence of metaphysical speculation. He has developed a Freudian complex with which to explain the internal life of the human being. Mystics, seers, saints, and visionaries, according to his way of thinking, are victims of self-delusion; they are obsessed by a God fixation.

Emerson has been described as a geographical misfit because he emerged as a mystic in a materialistic world, an idealist in a sphere of realists. Materialism has affected profoundly even the religious content in the average man. The moment we formalize a doctrine we condemn it to a condition of mortality. It is quite possible to maintain a belief in the reality of God and his angels and still be addicted to a basic materialism. It was the realization of this subtle point that drove Emerson from the Unitarian ministry. He could see that Christianity had been reduced to a system which demanded conformity to its doctrines and tenets. A man's Christianity is measured in terms of this conformity, and

Christian living is a discipline of obedience to the dictates of the Church rather than obedience to the dictates of the spirit.

In fairness to both viewpoints it is necessary to point out that it requires far more wisdom than is possessed by the average person to live well by the dictates of inner conviction alone. How shall we determine the demands of our spiritual natures, confused as we are by the internal babblings of emotion, sentiment, and desire? How shall we divide the false and true within ourselves? Like most intellectual idealists Emerson believed that other men shared the integrity of conviction which motivated him. Unfortunately, however, the average life is not devoted to thought and meditation, nor does it enjoy the profits of deep reading and wide travel. Emerson always found intimate contact with his fellow creatures disappointing and disillusioning, except for those rare instances in which he was privileged to mingle with his own kind. It is just as natural for the idealist to overestimate human nature as it is for the realist to underestimate the workings of man's consciousness.

All great systems of philosophy in which Emerson found his inspiration teach one essential doctrine. The substance of this doctrine is that the state of spiritual well-being results from the union of human nature with its own spiritual cause. This union is effected within the nature of the individual by his own effort and understanding, and credal affiliations hinder rather than help the process. God must be experienced spiritually and not merely accepted mentally.

The Oversoul

In his essay *The Oversoul* Emerson reveals to us the rare quality of his Neoplatonic vision. "We live in succession, in division, in parts, in particles. Meantime within man is the soul of the whole; the wise silence; the universal beauty to which every part and particle is equally related; the eternal One. And this deep power in which we exist, and whose beatitude is all accessible to us, is not only self-sufficing and perfect in every hour, but the act of seeing and the thing seen, the seer and the spectacle, the subject and the object, are one. We see the world piece by piece, as the sun, the moon, the animal, the tree; but the whole, of which these are the shining parts, is the soul. Only by the vision of that Wisdom can the horoscope of the ages be read, and by falling back on our better thoughts, by yielding to the spirit of prophecy which is innate in every man, we can know what it saith."

The recognition of the unity of life is the beginning of the mystical experience. Oneness is the supreme necessity. All parts must be subservient to pattern and to plan. They must depend upon a sovereign wholeness for their existence and their continuance. This is Platonism, the realization of the spiritual identity in all living creatures. Emerson calls the parent unity "that Oversoul, within which every man's particular being is contained and made one with all other..."

On this subject Emerson further reasons along classical lines: "All goes to show that the soul in man is not an organ, but animates and exercises all the organs; is not a function, like the power of memory, of calculation, of comparison, but uses these as hands and feet; is not a faculty, but a light; is not the intellect or the will, but the master of the intellect and the will; is the background of our being, in which they lie—an immensity not possessed and that cannot be possessed."

These are grand and noble thoughts for a man designed by tradition to be a New England clergyman. They justify us in assuming that he knew far more than he ever committed to writing. Here the philosopher emerges as a legitimate descendant of the Greek and Hindu sages whose imperishable thoughts are impelling the race toward the fulfillment of its own humanity.

The power of the oversoul is made manifest through the many channels of the personality. It comes through the man, but it is always greater than the man. Of the functions of the oversoul Emerson gives us a magnificent definition, "When it breathes through his intellect, it is genius; when it breathes through his will, it is virtue; when it flows through his affection, it is love. And the blindness of the intellect begins when it would be something of itself. The weakness of the will begins when the individual would be something of himself. All reform aims in some one particular to let the soul have its way through us; in other words, to engage us to obey."

The ancient Greeks believed the world soul to be the body of a blessed god in whom truly we live and move and have our being. This god inhabits a middle distance between spirit and matter and is revealed through the orders of creation. The material creation is not this soul, but bears witness to its power. To look upon nature is to behold the workings of the oversoul, for the unity of the world is the symbol of the unity that is behind the world.

The entire concept of the Messianic dispensation is grounded in the philosophy of the oversoul. The blessed God takes upon himself the illusion of the material sphere. The universal unity dies in matter and is reborn through mind. This is the myth of the dying god, the martyr spirit eternally sacrificing itself. The oversoul is the ever-coming spirit released through the ever-becoming of man.

Emerson distinguishes clearly between inspiration derived
from the soul and that which arises from external stimuli.
There are two kinds of philosophes, those who "speak *from
within* or from experience, as parties and possessors of the
fact," and those who "speak *from without* as spectators
merely, or perhaps as aquainted with the fact on the evidence
of third persons." This distinction which Emerson points
out is the real difference between classical and modern thinking. The sacred disciplines of the ancients were designed to
stimulate the growth of consciousness through the inward
experience of truth. The emphasis was upon the apperception of the working of God within the self. Modern intellectuals have an entirely different concept. To them philosophy is a mental exercise. The mind may be converted by
reason, argument, logic, or rhetoric, but there is no quicken-
ing of the spirit, no sense of unity with any larger self. The
drabness and wordiness of contemporary intellectuals result
from the utter lack of idealism or inspiration.

The law of compensation should never be confused with
the popular concept of retribution. The Hindu term *karma*
implies the impersonal working of the principle of cause and
effect. After attending a sermon in which the clergyman
assumed that injustice was inevitable in the material world,
and that only the last judgement could set things right,
Emerson was confirmed in his resolution to write an essay
on compensation.

In nature, moderation is the secret of survival. All extremes destroy themselves by the unbalance intrinsic in extremes. All excess results in deficiency; all deficiency leads
to excess. Poverty is a deficiency. Wealth is an excess, and
both are burdened by the absence of moderation. Governments that are cruel are overthrown. Laws that are unfair

impel reforms. We gain by losing, and lose by gaining. If we direct our attention to one subject we must abandon other interests and thus distort our characters. The penalty of achievement is fame. The penalty of failure is ignominy. The price of intemperance is pain, and the price of possession is loss. In life we achieve by selecting, and we pay for our selection by the absence of the qualities or things not selected. If we make music our life we may pine for art; if we select business as our career we languish for want of philosophy. When we accept a gift we usually inherit the giver, and in the end pay most for that which cost us nothing.

Opinions are a heavy burden upon the intellect. Every attitude has its compensation. We dislike; therefore we are disliked. We suspect; therefore we are suspected. We exploit; therefore we are exploited. Inordinate attachments lead to unreasonable grief, and dissolute habits corrupt the flesh. Nature has no place in her way of life for monopolies and exceptions, and throughout creation a universal tendency toward equalization is manifested.

Every attainment carries with it a burden of responsibility; every advance in station requires an increase of knowledge and skill; every privilege has its penalty; every reward its price. According to the ancient Cabala, "Unbalanced forces perish in the void." This is the law. The compensatory mechanism inherent in the creation itself cannot be denied its perfect works. Whether we will or no we must obey, and must accept the burden of action with the full realization of its inevitable consequences.

Emerson differs with the theologian who said that the good are miserable in the present life and the evil flourish exceedingly. He reasons thus: "What did the preacher mean...? Was it that houses and lands, offices, wine, horses, dress, luxury, are had by unprincipled men, while the saints are poor and despised; and that a compensation is to be made to these last hereafter, by giving them the like gratifications another day—bank-stocks and doubloons, venison and champagne? ... or to push it to its extreme import—'you sin now, we shall sin by and by; we would sin now, if we could; not being successful we expect our revenge tomorrow.'"

Psychology recognizes the existence of an autocorrective mechanism in the functioning processes of the human mind. As a man who feels himself falling instinctively throws his weight in the opposite direction, so the mind sensing that it is falling into a complex or fixation throws its force to a contrary extreme in an effort to maintain its balance. The mechanisms of escape belong in this category. The man who overtaxes his mind is impelled to frivolous recreations to the consternation of his associates. Mathematicians play the violin, and violinists dabble in mathematics. Left to its own devices, and unimpeded by the tyranny of self-will, the mental, emotional, and physical states of man are constantly striving for mutual concord among themselves, and for individual integrity in each of their several parts.

To the degree that the will tyrannizes over the personality the harmony of the nature is corrupted, and this corruption eventually frustrates the purposes of the will. So-called disaster is usually nothing but violent compensation set up by violent action. The causes are pleasant because we are following the dictates of our impulses and ambitions. The consequences are unpleasant because they are just payment for the injustices we have done to ourselves and others.

The poverty of the saints is a case in point. The natural compensation for holy living is the state of holiness. The heart and mind directed toward the mysteries of the spirit find strength and consolation in terms spiritual and mystical. There is nothing in nature to imply that an ascetic and pious existence is likely to result in physical opulence. Each tree bears its own fruit; those who live to acquire material wealth achieve their ends at the cost of their spiritual powers; those who live to attain spiritual wealth attain their ends at the cost of their material powers. This is not injustice, but compensation, for where a man's heart is there will be his treasure. Poverty is not the penalty of wisdom; it is the result of a standard of values. That which we regard as most valuable we will strive after, neglecting that which appears to be less valuable.

The Law of Compensation

The idea of retribution or punishment implies a despotism in nature by which we are punished for action. This is a superficial viewpoint. We are not made miserable for our sins but by our sinning. Compensation is intrinsic in action itself, and does not arise from the pressure of any arbitrary code set up in space by an irascible deity. In the last analysis compensation is not based upon a divine morality; rather human morality arises from experience grounded in the law of compensation. The compensatory impulse is present in every atom and molecule of the world. There is no creature in heaven or earth strong enough or great enough to defy this universal integrity. A man who casts himself from a high cliff expects to perish, and a man performing any action must expect the reaction appropriate to the causes which he has set in motion. Our senses incline us to believe that injustice is everywhere present, but when enlightenment dispels the illusions of the senses we realize that so-called injustice is but a pageantry of effects, the causes of which are unknown but entirely appropriate to the consequences which they have precipitated.

The law of compensation does not necessarily imply a principle of punishment. In each instance the end to be attained is constructive and beneficial. There is no vindictiveness in nature; only a sovereign justice moving eternally for the well-being of all creatures. If inordinate gain results in loss, so conversely, loss results in gain. All misfortune leads to a better state of fortune; all experience contributes to the growth of wisdom and the increase of understanding. No man is destroyed by the ills that befall him; rather he destroys himself by misinterpreting the edicts of natural law. We are not overcome by adversity but by the weakness in ourselves which cannot meet adversity with a good hope. There is no state of security toward which the human being aspires which cannot be attained if the causes of that security are set up within the individual himself. Compensation is not a law to be feared, for by the right use of this principle all that is desirable can be brought to pass.

The subject of universal law always brings the philosopher to the problem of fate and free will. In his essays on *The Conduct of Life* Emerson devotes the first section to this perplexing issue. "And, last of all," he writes, "high over thought, in the world of morals, Fate appears as vindicator, leveling the high, lifting the low, requiring justice in man, and always striking soon or late, when justice is not done." From his words it is evident that he identifies fate with the law of compensation. There is a fatality in the inevitable sequence of cause and consequence. Once the individual has devoted his mind to an enterprise, the rules governing that enterprise become the master of the man. His hopes, ambi-

tions, and fears, involved as they are in his project, dominate
his consciousness and impel the intellect to reason its way
through the confusion of the project to success or failure. If
fate administers all the works of man, free will remains to the
end the privilege of the man himself. He may choose and
decide, agree or disagree, accept or reject, but having once
cast his lot, having once reached the point of decision, fate
takes over and administers the rest.

Emerson's reasoning closely parallels the philosophy of
Gautama Buddha. There are two natures in man, the self,
which is ever free, and the not-self, which is forever bound.
The physical life of the human being is a fabrication of the
not-self and exists only because it is sanctified by the mortal
mind. Once this illusion is accepted as reality, the personality
is subject to its despotism. Having acknowledged the power
of the material world to limit the manifestations of consciousness, the individual becomes the hopeless prisoner of his
own conceit. On the plane of the not-self the world is
supreme and the laws governing the world are absolute in
authority.

The self dwells apart, patient and alone. It abides in the
condition of the universal, and recognizes no frustration or
inhibition of its eternal state. It is immovable and free and
beyond the laws governing motion; it is unchanging and free
beyond the laws governing change; it is unlimited and free
beyond the laws which impose limitation. On the plane of
the self there is neither cause nor consequence, no antagonism
between the universal in man and the universal in space.

"The day of days," writes Emerson, "the great day of the
feast of life, is that in which the inward eye opens to the
Unity in things, to the omnipresence of law." This is a
simple statement of the Buddhist doctrine of release. Man

became master not by the conquest of the world but by the conquest of his own not-self. Cause and effect end in perfect realization and perfect acceptance of the universal plan and the universal planner. Fate ceases its tyranny when consciousness transmutes the concept of fatal necessity into the conception of a splendid co-operation between the human being and the laws governing his existence.

The Beautiful Necessity

Our philosopher thus summarizes his vision of the cosmic pattern: "Why should we be afraid of nature, which is no other than 'philosophy, theology embodied'? Why should we fear to be crushed by savage elements, we who are made up of the same elements? Let us build to the Beautiful Necessity, which makes man brave in believing that he cannot shun a a danger that is appointed, nor incur one that is not; to the Necessity which rudely or softly educates him to the perception that there are no contingencies; that Law rules throughout existence, a Law which is not intelligent but intelligence, —not personal nor impersonal,—it disdains words and passes understanding; it dissolves persons; it vivifies natures, yet solicits the pure in heart to draw on all its omnipotence."

Emerson's opinions on wealth and private property can best be summarized by the simple statement that man is by constitution expensive. First nature requires that each man should feed himself. "If happily his fathers have left him no inheritance, he must go to work, and by making his wants less or his gains more, he must draw himself out of that state of pain and insult in which she forces the beggar to lie. She gives him no rest until this is done; she starves, taunts and torments him, takes away warmth, laughter, sleep, friends and daylight, until he has fought his way to his own loaf."

By temperament an aristocrat, Emerson, like Aristotle, saw no particular advantage in poverty. Believing that the philosopher, of all men, could make the best use of means, he urged the thinker to a practical course of life. The estate should be improved by honest and gainful occupation to the end that the thoughtful person may have an environment appropriate to the refinement of his taste. He sincerely believed that the struggle for economic security was part of the discipline of the soul. We are here to learn, and one of the most important of all the lessons is concentration.

Through the prodding of necessity the individual is forced to develop character, to learn patience in the presence of disaster, moderation in the presence of excess, gentleness in the presence of power, and Christian charity in the presence of a ruthless competitive system. There is no virtue in poverty unless it arises from the renunciation of worldly goods after success has been attained. Man is never rewarded for failure, and there is no merit in defending inability on the grounds of spiritual intent. We can renounce success but we cannot renounce failure or make it more powerful by doubting the negative.

Of course Emerson is referring to our civilization and the way of life into which Western peoples are born. His idealistic nature, seeking ever for the good in things as they are, realized the importance of the economic challenge. We are so temperamented that could we be happy without constant effort there would be no progress. Cheerfully we would settle back in a utopian indolence ending in complete demoralization. Our entire way of progress is motivated by the struggle for security. Art, science, religion, industry, and

trade are geared to a philosophy of expansion toward survival.
By constant diligence and prudence the mind is trained in a
sense of values, and it is this very training which reveals the
greater values which lie beyond competitive ethics. We outgrow the world by outgrowing the wordliness in ourselves.
We can escape from the limitations of our systems only by
becoming greater than those systems—never by evasion or
untrained revolt.

To outgrow means to unfold so much of self and the purposes of self that environment is overcome and its facilities
adapted to the requirements of the internal spiritual conviction. Emerson did not believe in a policy of protecting man
against his world, but rather in a program which preserved
the world from the evil works of man. This could come
only if the individual accepted personal responsibility and
lived in harmony with the laws of life. Man must win his
fight against internal and external limitation through the release of the talents and capacities locked within his being.
Right vision must impel to right action, and right action puts
the human state in order.

From these fragments of Emerson's philosophy it is easy
to see why academic thinkers have little time for either the
man or his work. They are not interested in disciplines of
conduct. They think for the sake of thought, regarding philosophy as an abstract means of weighing, estimating, comparing, and digesting the intellectual effort of other men. They
would dissect the body of learning in search of the disease
which destroyed the wisdom of the past. Having discovered
it they immediately develop similar symptoms in themselves,
falling from one error into another and passing on a legacy
of uncertainties to their scholastic issue.

Transcendentalism is the way of life of the idealistic philosopher. It would take noble thoughts and put them to work, molding character and building up integrity content. The end of mature thinking is intellectual serenity, the courage to live well, and the skill to defend the dignity of the indwelling divinity from the encroachment of doubts, fears, and inordinate desires. Mysticism is living from within toward the circumference of action. Philosophy sets up the machinery by which inner consciousness gains complete control over condition and circumstance.

Young men starting out in life are apt to select dynamic philosophies like those of Nietzsche and Schopenhauer. They are more interested in the will to power than the will to peace. It is only after actual living has mellowed ambition and deepened the emotions that these same men, older now, begin to appreciate the maturity of Emerson's idealism. We seek power in the outer world, but for peace we must search within. When the mind becomes aware of this eternal truth idealistic philosophy becomes for each of us the "Beautiful Necessity."

8

THE NEOPLATONIC RESTORATION

A Review

THE transcendent beauty of the Platonic philosophy has won the universal admiration of mankind. The writings of Plato and the more illustrious of his followers have been translated into all the principal languages of the world, and have influenced the intellectual, cultural, and ethical standards of the entire race.

Though the ethical integrity of the Platonic viewpoint has never been seriously questioned, the Aristotelians, in particular, have pointed out what they call deficiency of method in the doctrines of the great master. By deficiency of method these critics imply that while Platonism visualizes the ideal state, it fails utterly to provide a mechanism for the achievement of that state. Certain reformations are advanced as necessary. The advantages to be attained by these changes are clearly pointed out, but the means by which the present state of human nature may be adapted to these reformations is not given or even implied. Because of this apparent weakness in the basic texts, Platonism has been stigmatized as impractical, a noble vagary evidently true but obviously impossible of application.

The deficiency of method is an essential point of difference between a philosophy and a religion. The primary point of philosophy is to expound reasonable facts and to reveal these facts intellectually; that is, so that they are understandable and acceptable to the intellect. The moment a machinery is set up with an elaborate structure of moral and ethical recommendations, philosophy verges toward religion, and even theology.

We can see an outstanding example of this mingling of conflicting premises in the story of Indian Buddhism. Gautama Buddha was a philosopher, and from the evidence of the earliest available records of his teachings, an agnostic. He refused to discuss the nature of God, agreeing with the Socratic viewpoint that all efforts to reduce the incomprehensible to the limitations of human thinking were both unreasonable and unprofitable. Yet Buddhism emerges as the great religion of Asia. Around its simple premises has been built up an elaborate structure of religious symbolism, mystical speculation, ritualism, and sacerdotalism in general.

The rise of Platonism was blocked by the advent of the Christian faith. A strong religious principle emerged from the Near East and North Africa, and as it increased the pagan philosophies were correspondingly submerged. Had a new faith not arisen it is quite probable that Platonism and Neoplatonism would have become the religion of the West. As it is, much of the best of the Platonic teaching was incorporated into the structure of the Church, as we have already noted.

The combination of pagan purpose and Christian method deserves critical analysis; in fact, the great dilemma of the Church has been the problem of method. The brotherhood of man, for example, is a noble concept held equally by both philosophy and religion, yet neither of these institutions has been able to perfect its conviction in terms of method. Even the untutored multitudes are inclined to view a fraternity of human purpose as desirable, but neither the individual nor the collective group has been able to demonstrate the cherished belief that human beings should be united in the essentials of living. In spite of our every resolution, co-operation verges inevitably toward corporation.

The Search for Security

If it is held against Platonism that it is devoid of method, it may be held against Aristotelianism that although abounding in method it has never been able to apply its machinery successfully in the sphere of material ambition. The human mind in its search for security and material success refuses to limit its opportunities or its philosophy of opportunism by any ethical restraints upon freedom of action.

After pondering the Platonic and Neoplatonic institutes for a number of years, it seems to me that the supreme proof of Plato's genius is that he refrained from imposing the limitations of method upon the universality of his convictions. It is not because his mind was deficient in this respect; rather, he realized that the formality of method defeats its own ends by obscuring all ends with the burden of means. We know that in religion means have become ends, and that in addiction to means we find a false security. It is the emphasis upon means which has brought about what the Platonists might have called the privation of ends, or as the sociologists might describe as the ends of privation.

When Aristotle, contemplating the great ideals of his master, became aware of the qualitative interval between the divine above and the human below, he attempted to bridge this lacuna with categories of methods. Unfortunately, all he could do was build another Tower of Babel. Instead of facilitating the course of idealism, he imprisoned universals in bodies fashioned of mathematical intellectualism.

Gentle Plato was the wiser man. He knew from his own experience that method belongs to time and place, but truth is timeless and beyond the limitation of place. Man must eternally seek for that which is eternal, but method changes with the seasons. The pattern that serves one generation is useless in another. An ethical machinery may inspire for a certain time, and then the machinery becomes obsolete. If the abstract ideals have come to be identified with any system or method they perish when that method fails. Method is a kind of body, and ideals are the spirit which inhabits that body. It is fatal to progress to regard the body as identical with its indwelling spirit. All bodies are corruptible, but spirits are incorruptible. Plato sought to preserve the immortality of truth by refusing to permit its incarnation within a machinery of utility.

Aristotle desired to fashion again the Homeric golden chain which bound the material world to the throne of Olympian Zeus. He would bind God and nature with eternal bonds. The categories are the links of his golden chain. They achieve everything except their final purpose, which is the creation from nature of the god-man, the philosopher-king.

The quiet tolerance of Plato, his gentle patience with Aristotle's spiritual ambitions, were typical of the characters of the two men. Plato was patient because patience is the only way. Growth cannot be forced. We can contribute to progress, but we can never insist successfully that our contributions be accepted. We can point out the end to be attained, but we must also understand that each human being must attain this end in his own way, through his own experience and his own necessity in his own time and in his own place.

Plato had no dispute with Aristotle, for it was Aristotle himself who was the moving spirit in his own disputations. Plato knew that when his disciple argued with others it was because in reality the young man was arguing with himself. We are eternally seeking the conversion of others as a means of achieving or sustaining the conversion of ourselves. Aristotle was a truth seeker, and Plato realized that this brilliant intellect was attaining the very end which the master desired. Aristotle had accepted the challenge of the absence of method, which was exactly what Plato wanted him to do and what Platonism has invited all thoughtful persons to attempt since the first presentation of the doctrine.

Plato appears to have learned from his own master, Socrates, that in the processes of thinking the most desirable end is that the student or disciple shall learn to think for himself. He must work out his own form, and if in this procedure he feels, as Aristotle did, that he is correcting a grave fault in his master's teachings, so much the better. It is better to find fault and think than it is to agree perfectly and accept the thoughts of others.

The impact of Plato upon Aristotle proves the efficacy of the Platonic method. Aristotle became a leader and not a follower. He created his own world by releasing the qualities of his own mind. Had Plato forced upon him a complete machinery of method, Aristotle's name would not have survived.

Plato was able to accomplish his purpose because he was too advanced as a philosopher to be limited by the implications of his own ego. It is comforting to small minds to have followers, and to force others into agreement with the patterns which the egotist himself has revealed to a wondering and admiring world. It requires a higher measure of greatness to refrain from dominating the intellectual processes of others. To be quiet while they disagree, and to inwardly rejoice because this disagreement represents sincere effort to think for oneself, is the better part of wisdom. It is said that Plato had a peculiarly mild, almost vacant expression in those moments when his doctrines were being assailed by some enthusiastic intellectual. This mask was truly Socratic. Plato would listen like some kindly grandfather, never reproving nor reproaching, and permitting his adversary to feel that the master was utterly overwhelmed at the show of erudition. It is probable that some of the disciples were a little disappointed that the master did not immediately alter the whole fabric of his philosophy in favor of their improvements, but Plato kept on, listening, nodding, beaming, and teaching exactly as he had taught before.

Universal Being exists as both time and eternity. Being, in terms of time, is a motion of life from things previous to things subsequent. This motion is visible to us through the growth and unfoldment of forms. Forms exist in time and in place, and are measured in terms of these dimensions.

That part of Universal Being which exists beyond the limitation of time may be said to subsist by virtue of its own existence without dependence upon any antecedent cause beyond itself. Eternity generates time, but is itself timeless. It generates motion, but is itself motionless. It is the apex of causes, yet is without cause. It is the source of division, yet is undivided. Eternity is of the nature of ends which are indivisible because they cannot be defined. For example, through the practice of the virtues we may attain the substance of the virtuous. Virtues may be defined and distinguished according to time and place, but the substance of *the virtuous* cannot be defined, nor can the intellect set up division within the measure of this term. Or again, beauty is subject to definition according to taste, cultivation, and circumstance, but *the beautiful* is not to be distinguished in its absolute substance.

Applying these abstract principles to the Platonic teaching it becomes obvious why Plato emphasized ends rather than means. There is a subtle point here. The motion of means is inevitably toward ends, a motion of dissimilars toward identity. In terms of philosophy, wisdom is an end, and all learning is a means to that end. We may define learning in terms of arts and sciences, crafts and trades, professions and vocations; we may select from these such as are suitable to our dispositions, and through diligent application progress our natures toward the state of wisdom. We all aspire to the attainment of wisdom, although the most audacious mortals would hesitate to attempt a definition of wisdom. Yet undefined and beyond even intellectual dimensions, wisdom is regarded universally as desirable above all the treasures of the earth. There is no uniformity of opinion regarding means or method, each department of learning claiming precedence and all departments subject to renovation according to time and place.

Means are dominated by the concept of the known, but ends are composed of the known plus the unknown. The mind can outgrow the means, but cannot outgrow the end, for it contains both that which is attained and that which is attainable. Thus growth is forever in conflict with means but in concord with ends.

Aristotle, by attempting to systematize means, sought to pave a road to ends. He took into account a variety of natural laws but appears to have overlooked one cardinal tenet of universal procedure—the law of change. In nature nothing is changeless but change. The alchemical minglings of time and place engender an endless variety of mutable appearances. Ever-moving patterns acting upon each other challenge the existence of each creature that inhabits the natural diffusion.

Man himself consists of two natures. Spiritually he is a part of the universe and partakes of eternity, thus sharing in the permanence of ends. Materially he partakes of time and place, and thus participates in the impermanence of means. From this circumstance there arises a conflict within himself. As material evolution is measured by the growth and refinement of the personality, spiritual evolution is measured by the victory of ends over means as an experience of consciousness. This was the peculiar doctrine of the Neoplatonists. The arts and sciences can be mastered, but wisdom cannot be mastered. Knowledge can be possessed, but truth cannot be possessed. Beauty can be captured by the artist, but the beautiful is forever free. Thus the individual can possess means, but ends possess the individual.

Plato's Political Philosophy

When Plato, through the lips of Socrates, describes the government of the philosophic elect he reveals the end of government. He tells us that no particular system, by virtue of being a system, will ever attain this end. He emphasizes the corruptions common to all systems by which the desirable end is frustrated.

Monarchy degenerates into tyranny, oligarchy degenerates into bureaucracy, and democracy falls into chaos. All systems fail if abused. All can succeed if administered by the wise. To be wise, therefore, is the only remedy for the numerous diseases of ignorance, and nothing is to be gained by the substitution of one inadequacy for another. Why then set up a new machinery for the same corruption to inherit? Why substitute words for ideas, names for facts, and political parties for the laws of government? Systems have no real substance in themselves. They are ensouled by their partisans, vitalized and devitalized by their adherents. Ignorance is forever changing its name, but by any name it is still ignorance.

Plato retired from active participation in Athenian politics because he realized that the governmental machinery of the city made impossible the just administration of the laws. Yet this machinery had been set up by able men devoted to the common good and vigorously opposed to corruption. Wherein, then, lay the fault? The answer was obvious; self-seeking politicians had found a way to outwit the spirit of good laws and at the same time preserve the letter and their own safety.

In this dilemma upright citizens rose up crying out for reform. If they succeeded in overthrowing the incumbent party, those cast down rose up again demanding that the reformers be reformed. Thus the wheel of fortune turns upon the spindle of necessity, and nothing appears consistent but corruption and high taxes.

All men desired better government but few could agree as to what constituted better government. Each had a method but these methods had little in common save confusion. All men desired perfection but were in violent conflict as to the definition of perfection. Private interest and public good were irreconcilable.

In religion the same dilemma prevailed. All men agreed on the existence of a supreme principle appropriately termed God, but men could not agree upon any definition of Deity, nor could they find common ground in private or public worship. Each frequented a shrine or sanctuary of his own selection, and worshiped the Supreme One with a variety of rituals and ceremonies. Here again there was unity in ends, but no unity in methods. In fact, disunity of methods resulted in open conflict and recurrent cycles of cruelty and oppression in the name of an all-loving God.

Even in Plato's time there was no lack of method in religion. The temples were the custodians of esoteric sciences intended to cultivate or perfect the spiritual content in human nature. The priests of these temples were men of noble character and high philosophic attainment. But even these sublime institutions were unable to prevent internal strife among the states of Greece, or wars with neighboring countries. It was not lack of method that prevented the brotherhood of man; it was the inability of the human being to escape from the practice of means to the realization of ends. This inadequacy was in man himself and not in his institutions, and against this inadequacy the optimism of method was insufficient.

In the two thousand years that have passed since the decline of the classical schools the situation has remained comparatively unchanged. The modern world still clings tenaciously to the significance of method. We still believe that we can set up a machinery that will result in the preservation and perfection of the race. For this enthusiastic conviction we are certainly indebted to Aristotle. He is an outstanding example of the disastrous results of clinging to a fixed standard in a moving universe. There are occasions when we are false to the future if we cling to the past.

We must be careful, however, not to dogmatize even upon a generality of this kind. We must not think of the past in terms of fixation. Plato belongs to the past in time, but to the future in the eternity of his vision. By building no walls, by placing no limitation upon mental or physical progress, Plato has held the respect of mankind by releasing man from any bondage to doctrine or opinion. That which is without limitation is without date, but that which is limited is inevitably dated.

The Platonic viewpoint deserves the admiration of a sorely troubled world because it is the only philosophy of the West that is actually solutional. It cannot be outgrown, because its proportions and dimensions were never fixed. There can never be a discovery in the world of science, a vision in the world of art, or a conviction in the world of religion, that is not Platonic. Plato's unknown quantity in the substance of being is an infinite capacity into which human endeavor can pour the works of its genius to the end of time. Discovery only reveals more of that which eternally is. This was the greatness of the man, and of that other man who lived in Asia three hundred years earlier, Gautama Buddha. Both of these great philosophers built their systems upon a conception of infinite progress. Their systems can be denied or ignored, but they can never be disproved or outgrown. Both allowed for infinite growth in their scheme of things, and neither suspended his doctrine from a machinery that could be discredited.

Because Platonism is without those formal boundaries which we have come to demand as essential to the structure of belief, we regard his teachings as vague and difficult of comprehension. After all, truth and wisdom, virtue and beauty, love and integrity, are all words to express ideas not exactly concrete. We are forever creating definitions for these words, identifying the idea with the definition for a time, and ultimately rejecting the definition as unworthy of the idea. If Plato is vague it is because the infinite itself is beyond definition and delineation.

The cause of the dilemma is obvious, but the remedy is extremely difficult of attainment. Man lives in a finite world and his faculties are limited to that sensory sphere of which his bodies are a part. How can the finite measure the Infinite? How can we understand that which is totally beyond our experience, and how can we experience that which is beyond the range of our perceptions? This line of reasoning seems to end against a blank wall. To know more than we do know we must become greater than we are now. To be greater than we are now we must know more than we know now. Is it any wonder, then, that so many modern philosophers are addicted to extreme pessimism?

It remained for the Neoplatonists of Alexandria to project the metaphysical speculations of Plato to their reasonable conclusions. This projection resulted in the development of a new department within the compound structure of philosophy. This new department was theurgy, a union of philosophy and mysticism. We can never know to what degree Plato attained this union, for his mystical writings have not survived. Certainly the projection of philosophy toward theurgy was entirely reasonable and consistent with the whole structure of the Orphic theology.

There was an oriental precedent for the setting up of theurgy as a method to break the circle of cause and consequence. Buddha had already done this by creating the discipline of realization by which the human being could free himself from the wheel of the law. Realization was the escape toward the self; a scientific organization of the powers of consciousness for the purpose of releasing the internal eternity of man from bondage to the limitations of time and place. In simple terms, it was the restatement as conscious experience of reality over illusion. The theurgy of Neoplatonism was motivated by the same internal requirements, and sought to accomplish identical results.

Spiritual evolution required that the circle of life be broken without violating the cyclic motion inherent in the laws of life. To change the circle into an ascending cycle it was necessary to introduce the concept of the spiral, an ascending circle without limitation. A spiral motion might appear to bring about an infinite repetition of circumstances or occurrences. Yet in spite of similarity there could be no identity. Repetition occurred upon an ascending scale, each apparent recurrence differing in quality from that which had preceded it. The circumstance might be altered by time or place in terms of externals, or by state or condition in terms of internals. Thus a man may repeat the same action day after day, but each repetition will be marked by a gradually ascending scale of proficiency or skill gained from practice. More than this, the man himself grows, and though he repeats the action he himself increases from day to day so that neither the action nor the person acting is precisely the same on any two occasions.

Theurgy unfolds the mystery of qualitative interval and seeks to set up a method for bridging the chasm of quality. This it accomplishes by gradually releasing universal consciousness through the unfolding faculties and functions of the human being. This science of approaching universals is the master science of the Ancient Mysteries.

If we apply Plato's three categories of the nature of being to the subject of intellect, we arrive at some interesting conclusions. Plato divided all living creatures into three orders: the unmoved, the self-moved, and the moved. The unmoved is spirit, the self-moving is intellect, and the moved is form or body.

In the sphere of mind the unmoved is wisdom, the self-moving is science or knowledge, and the moved is opinion. Therefore the ascent from opinion to science may be defined as the establishment of a self-moving intellect. By this means the individual accomplishes the triumph of the personal self over circumstances. This may be further defined as orientation; the discovery of the place of the personal self in the theater of conditions.

From Science to Wisdom

The end of science is thus revealed to consist not in the sciences but in the self. The individual does not live to advance learning; he learns to advance living. Science is not an end but a means; the natural defense against the dangers of opinion. It is not correct to say that man possesses opinions, for in the sphere of opinion, it is opinions that obsess man. In this state the human being is the victim of externals; not only his own opinions which are external to the self, but others opinions, which are external to the body. By the attainment of self-motion (science) the individual becomes master of opinion by subjecting it to the disciplines of the reason. Science is in this instance a kind of sieve. The mathematical sieve of Eratosthenes, invented about 230 B. C., is an appropriate example. By means of this device composite and incomposite odd numbers could be sifted from the sequence of numbers. By science, perfect, superabundant, and deficient fact may be sifted fom the sequence of opinion.

The ascent from science to wisdom is, according to this system of analogy, voluntary motion of the self-moving toward the substance of the unmoved. It is the ascent of the mind from facts of the intellect to certainties of the consciousness. Let us consider the nature of fact as it applies to the present problem. Fact is a thing demonstrably and undeniably true. It is a fact that rain falls, that plants grow, that creatures exist and that darkness follows light in the phenomenon of day and night. These obvious truths may be defined in the sieve of learning as *deficient fact*. The deficiency results from the static nature of this kind of fact. Most knowledge as we know it today consists of deficient fact. The deficiency is proved by the circumstance that this kind of fact can be amassed without changing the state of man. He may possess these facts and still remain ignorant concerning his own nature, the reason for his existence, and the relationship between himself and these facts. Such facts are sterile truths, undeniable but insufficient.

Superabundant fact is the fact itself surrounded by an aura of implications. These implications are reasonable extensions of the fact itself toward utility. If the extension of the fact is downward, the result is the application of principles to the various machineries set up in material life. This extension results in the application of principles (facts) to the requirements of industry, economics, and human security in general.

If the extension of the fact is upward, it stimulates certain inventiveness and originality of the reason by which the secuity of the internal self is achieved. The upward extension of superabundant or dynamic fact toward union with consciousness is the province of philosophy. The seventh and highest branch of philosophy is theurgy, which is the esoteric art of binding superabundant fact to its own cause, perfect fact, or being.

Perfect fact is the unmoved mover of the mind. It is unmoved because it cannot depart from the nature of itself. It is the mover because it draws all intellect to itself by divine fascination. The search for perfect fact is the proper exercise of the intellect. The quest for perfect fact becomes what the Greeks called a frenzy of the spirit. The intellectual appetite cannot be satisfied until it beholds and receives unto itself the light of Universal Truth. This is the passion of the soul for union with its own substance. The substance itself is immovable, and all motion takes place within beings deficient of perfect fact and resolutely determined to make the journey to Self.

The recognition of superabundant fact brings with it the realization of the superiority of that which exists by the nature of being, over that which exists by the nature of appearance. The center of reality is shifted from the focus of form to the focus of principles behind form. The invisible, according to the substance of principle, takes precedence over the visible which subsists according to the nature of bodies.

The sphere of science (superabundant fact) is divided into an upper and lower hemisphere. The lower, or dark hemisphere, is fact superabundant in terms of exactitude. This is exactitude as contrasted to opinion, and by this contrast proved to be superior. Exactitude implies thoroughness but not necessarily extension upward to imponderables. The lower hemisphere of science is properly termed materialistic, for it is the mover of things inferior to itself, giving the mind dominion over bodies but not dominion over the principles resident in bodies.

The upper hemisphere of science is properly defined as idealistic, for it impels the intellect toward the search for cause. All cause is by nature both real and invisible, and it cannot be approached until the mind is able to accept the reality of things invisible and the power of the invisible as governor of all visible manifestations. Thus by its own nature the upper hemisphere of science contains the ingredients of a philosophic viewpoint, and gently urges the intellect to search for those secret causes which the ancients referred to as the gods of several orders.

The search for perfect fact can only be accomplished by the unfoldment of internal capacities. To perceive that which is beyond matter requires faculties beyond the material. Awareness is necessary to the condition of being aware. The refinement of faculty results in the extension of the powers of the faculties in the sphere of intangibles. Mental evolution is the unfoldment of the faculties of consciousness toward the apprehension or apperception of consciousness per se; it is as though we increased in truthfulness until we shared in the substance of truth itself.

All human growth results from discipline. Opinions themselves discipline the opinionated. This may be defined as growth by adversity. The consequences of opinionism become unendurable, and the intellect seeks to escape from the net of circumstances by the use of mental images. Once the mind comes into control it must be trained to become the leader of the personality. This is the purpose of education. All education converges to the center of science, which seeks

to equip the mind for dominion over body. The end of the
process is the victory of purpose over accident.

As the mind requires a long process of direction and control before it is sufficient to the requirements of personality,
it requires further discipline before it is capable of sustaining
the philosophic over-life. The ascent from science to philosophy is only possible to those who accept the disciplines of
philosophy and make these disciplines their way of living.

In the modern world philosophy has come to be regarded
as a superabundant intellectualism. The mind has attempted
to impose its own patterns upon all of nature, visible and invisible. Materialistic philosophy is little better than a cautious
step from the scientific center. There is little courage in the
philosophic convictions of this century, and still less inclination to regard philosophy as a way of life and not merely
an intellectual exercise.

It is difficult to define the power or faculty of realization
as it manifests in man. Certainly it is apperceptive estimation; it is a knowledge of things from and within themselves.
Possibly the best term is participation. In life the individual
can be either an observer or a participant. As an observer
he is apart from the substance of the thing observed. He is
a beholder of life, capable of analyzing and classifying things
seen but having no part in things known. The participant
has an entirely different point of view. He experiences circumstance as a part of himself; he shares in the experience
and feels the flow of it through his own consciousness.

In the philosophic world the materialistic thinker remains
an observer of the universal plan. He is untouched by the
impact of personal experience. The idealistic philosopher
aspires to a participation in the consciousness which moves
the worlds and manifests through the intricate pattern of uni-

versal laws. The conviction that it is possible for the human being to so participate in the substance of the divine plan is properly termed mysticism. The technique by which the human personality may be disciplined for such participation was called by the Neoplatonists the theurgic art.

There is no actual proof that Plato himself defined a theurgic discipline, but it certainly originated from a contemplation of his conception of universals as they apply to the state of mankind. Without theurgy philosophy ends in a hypocritical intellectual materialism. There is no escape for the mind except upward and inward toward the fountain of the self.

The materialist regards evolution as a gradual process requiring vast periods of time, and subject to innumerable natural accidents. There is no promise of perfection for any species or kind. Survival is a matter of circumstances. If survival is accomplished it will be accompanied by a growth of the potentials within the surviving form. But the earth beneath our feet is a graveyard of extinct forms which lost the struggle for survival. The evolution of forms is an insufficient doctrine unless consideration is given to the life principles which ensoul forms, and which are the true sources of the growth apparent in formal structures.

The psychosomatic theory of medicine has discovered the existence of a person within the body. As yet this person is regarded as a kind of overtone; a complex of the body itself, incapable of independent survival. But a wedge has been driven into what has been regarded as an indissolvable compound. Time will certainly bring about a recognition of the reality of the internal man, and prove that the man is the reality and the body is the extension.

The descent of the Platonic theology has resulted in an unbroken line of idealistic philosophers, all of whom have held, to some degree, the reality of Divine Being and Divine Laws operating behind and through the veil of matter. The spiritual is the real, and the material is the extension of that reality from itself toward its own circumference. This circumference is called the privation because in it the universal reality reaches its ultimate degree of obscuration. Ignorance, for example, is not a substance nor a principle; it is the privation of wisdom. By the same analogy darkness is the privation of light; error is the privation of truth; death is the privation of life; and to a degree, man is the privation of God.

Boehme describes privation as hunger, an insatiable appetite demanding nutrition. Thus man hungers for God, and the whole machinery of his purpose is directed toward the satisfaction of his appetite. The mystic is one who hungers after righteousness, and his soul can never find rest until it experiences the presence of the Divine Power. False appetites may obscure temporarily the true purpose for living, but stress and adversity restore the normal appetite and press the personality onward to the attainment of that which is most necessary.

Nearly all of the Platonic philosophers recognize mathematics as the most perfect of the sciences. By meditating upon the arithmetical progression of numbers the consciousness becomes aware of the orderly extension of the divine nature throughout the worlds. Mathematics bestows an internal certainty about the plan or pattern of existence. Properly understood, the science of numbers overcomes the concept of accident. The human being finds himself in a framework of orderly procedure. He perceives the world to be the extension of the Divine Consciousness in terms of perfect reason, perfect wisdom, and perfect love.

Having realized that the universe is in order, man is forced to the natural conclusion that if disorder exists it is in himself and not in the world. This realization is sufficient to indicate the correct remedy for the prevailing uncertainties.

The rise of the Christian Church resulted in a dramatic conflict of ideologies. Pagan philosophy was built upon a broad and comparatively tolerant foundation. The ancients knew very little about the idea of heresy. Beliefs were examined according to content rather than according to form. Men were respected for the quality of their ideas and not for their allegiance to particular schools or sects. Dogmas and doctrines were accepted as means rather than ends, and there was a universal tolerance toward method so long as method accomplished meritorious results.

The early Christian Church threw most of its weight upon means and demanded uniformity of technique as well as identity of purpose. By the glorification of means, ends were obscured, and religion became identified with the theological institutes through which it manifested. With theology as a primary concern, religion was relegated to second place in the scale of ecclesiastical values. The sanctification of method is the vital ingredient in the compound of dogma.

Hypatia of Alexandria

No consideration of the conflict between Neoplatonism and the early Christian Church could be complete without reference to the splendid character of Hypatia of Alexandria. In her personality we have an outstanding instance of the tragedy arising from the impact of theology upon a liberal philosophical idealism—the last surviving institution of classical pagan intellectualism. Hypatia was the daughter of Theon, the mathematician whose learning had gained for him a distinguished position of leadership in the Alexandrian school. It should be noted that the term mathematician inferred much more than skill in arithmetic. Theon, and others of similar attainment, were Platonists developing abstract idealistic convictions according to orderly procedures revealed through the study of geometry and mathematics.

Theon wrote extensive and learned commentaries on Euclid and Ptolemy, and it is believed that his talented daughter assisted him in a number of his writings. Hypatia lectured on astronomy, physics, and mathematics, and according to Suidas prepared an elaborate gloss on the *Arithmetica* of Diophantus.

After the death of Theon, Hypatia attained his chair in the school and rose to be the principal exponent of Neoplatonism in Egypt. Her achievements were the more remarkable when we realize that although many women of classical antiquity were brilliantly educated, few reached public prominence. So profound was her intellect and so outstanding her eloquence that she attracted a brilliant group of disciples, including Synesius, who later became a 'nominal' Christian and was elected Bishop of Ptolemais.

Synesius accepted the dignity and responsibility of leadership in the North African Church only after the Fathers had agreed to certain stipulations which this conscientious disciple of Neoplatonic discipline demanded. First, his private addiction to Greek metaphysical speculation must be respected, and second, he should be permitted to retain his wife with whom he had lived happily the greater part of his life. The Church permitted Synesius to remain a pagan in his inward parts, so the conversion was a marked success.

Even after his appointment as bishop Synesius frequently consulted Hypatia on scientific problems. He required her assistance in the construction of an astrolabe and a hydroscope; the former a device for determining the ascension of stars, indispensable to navigation at that time, and the latter a clock motivated by water. It never occurred to Synesius that the religion which a man professed could interfere with the furtherance of his intellectual pursuits, and he could not conceive of intellectuals prejudiced by religious convictions. For him learning was where he found it.

Hypatia was born in Alexandria about A. D. 370, and had the misfortune to live in the midst of the conflict raging throughout North Africa and the Near East between the classical pagan schools and the rising power of the early Christian Church. Neither the beauty and modesty of her person, nor the depth of her scholarship, could protect her from the fanaticism of the times. An infuriated mob of Christian converts incited by Peter the Reader, a fanatical and unlearned man, dragged her from her chariot, forced her into the Caesareum which was then a Christian Church, stripped her clothes from her body and hacked her to death with oyster shells. The excuse given was that she enjoyed the protection of Orestes, the prefect of Alexandria, who was a pagan and a thorn in the flesh of Cyril, surnamed The Good, the Christian patriarch. Cyril also attacked the Jewish synagogues with forces of armed men, and it was his militant intolerance which brought him into conflict with Orestes, who desired to maintain a tolerant attitude in matters of personal belief. Hypatia has survived in the hagiology of the Roman Catholic Church in the person of St. Catherine of Alexandria.

Deep issues were involved in the martyrdom of Hypatia. The early Church was developing a fantastic antipathy for learning and the intellectual individualism which learning bestowed. Sciences such as astronomy, geography, chemistry, and even medicine were denounced as madness or tolerated only because the Church was not strong enough to destroy them. Books and manuscripts were destroyed on every hand, and the mere possession of the mathematical text was sufficient to condemn a family to death. In Rome, Gregory the Great expelled all mathematicians from the Holy City, and burned the Palatine Library which had been founded by Augustus Caesar. Mathematics in particular was the victim of theological abuse, and Hypatia was a martyr to the multiplication table. She died in March A. D. 415 and her school perished for lack of her guiding spirit.

In our day when religion has come to be regarded as an emotional experience in the life of the human being, and when faith is belief in the substance of things unseen, unknown, and unproved, it is difficult to visualize a religious conviction founded in philosophical and scientific disciplines. We may accept the doubtful hypothesis that faith bestows wisdom, but we deny the wholly reasonable hypothesis that wisdom bestows faith. Bacon stated the matter expertly when he affirmed that great learning brings the mind to God.

To the ancients, religious belief was a conviction resulting from a scientific contemplation of causes. The mind discovered God through the contemplation of universal principles and the manifestations which these principles set up in the sphere of particulars. All learning impels the consciousness to the acceptance of an abiding Divinity which dwells in the furthermost and the innermost. It is because idealistic learning impels the intellect toward the acknowledgment of Eternal

Being that Platonism is properly regarded as both a philosophy and a religion. The purpose of learning is to discover the nature of Being as cause. Thus true learning must in the end lead to faith, and faith, by this definition, is acceptance (as an experience in consciousness) of the spiritual foundations of the material world.

Leadership in nature is the privilege of superiors. If leadership is entrusted to inferiors, confusion is inevitable. That which excels in merit is truly superior and that which is deficient in merit is unsuited for superior estate. Obviously, wisdom is superior to ignorance, for ignorance, as a state, is deficient in a primary requisite—sufficiency. Ignorant persons require leadership in order to survive. Wise persons however, do not require ignorance for the preservation of themselves; therefore ignorance is not requisite, and that which is not requisite is not necessary, and that which is not necessary is subservient or less than that which is necessary. The only art, science, or trade which can be furthered by ignorance is despotism. Wisdom is desirable because it is a general prerequisite to the attainment of any particular. A wise man is skillful in knowing, and skill is a combination of knowledge and discipline. The primary end of philosophy is the attainment of wisdom, or the state of knowing. Knowledge is of three kinds: the knowledge of things, of self, and of the gods. To set up a relative pattern it can be said that knowledge of things is scientific knowledge; the knowledge of self is philosophic knowledge, and knowledge of the gods is spiritual knowledge. Deficiency of knowledge in any of these departments results in the state of ignorance.

We have attempted to unfold in this book the extensions of a philosophical pattern through an order of creative thinkers. Idealistic philosophy, through its legitimate disciples, has been applied to the organization of the rational faculties of the human being for the solution of man's common necessity, the need of wisdom. The Neoplatonic program is one of the gradual ascent through conditions of relative knowing to the ultimate state of absolute knowing. Here classical philosophy comes into conflict with the basic conviction of the modern world; namely, that absolute knowledge is impossible.

The Knowledge of Causes

An examination of the dimensions and implications of the term absolute knowledge is indicated at this point in our analysis. As all knowledge ends in the knowledge of causes, it must follow that the knowledge of causes is absolute knowledge. But are causes identical either in quality or quantity? Do they exist in one place or in many places? If causes are identical, how does it occur that identity projects nonidentity; that is, how can a unity of cause produce a diversity of effect? If causes are not identical, have they a common denominator beyond cause?

The Aristotelians escape from the dilemma of first or absolute cause by postulating the eternity of the world. That which is eternal is without beginning or end, and exists in the quality of continuance. Yet all visible natures have beginning and end, and all effects in nature are suspended from causes, and become in turn causes producing effects.

In terms of Platonism, the inability of the intellect to apprehend causes is due to the natural deficiencies of the reasoning powers. If absolute cause exists, it abides beyond the radius of intellectual energy. If cause is of the nature of mind it can be discovered by the mind, but if cause is something different from mind it cannot be known or experienced by the mind.

If the mind cannot command the nature of cause, one of two conclusions is inevitable. Either the nature of cause is utterly unknowable, or it must be discovered by a faculty superior to mind. If we deny the existence of a superior faculty, we deny at the same time that the human being ever can know the causes of the world and himself. To be ignorant of cause is to be utterly frustrated in the estimation of effects. Unless we understand where we came from, why we are here, and where we are going, there is no way in which we can advance our own destiny. We cannot obey the unknowable, nor can we achieve a state of security if there is no way to orient ourselves in the universal pattern. We can exist only from day to day, burdened internally by an absolute frustration and obsessed by an emotion of complete defeatism.

The term absolute, when applied to cause, has a special meaning to the Platonic metaphysician. He recognizes qualities in causation. There may be absolute cause abiding in absolute space, and there may also be absolute cause in the midst of the solar system or a planet or in man himself. The absolute cause of a thing is the cause of the wholeness of that thing as distinguished from those secondary causes which refer to the motions and relations of parts. Thus the human spirit is the absolute cause of man. The world spirit is the absolute cause of the world. And the universal spirit is the absolute cause of the universe. The spirit of a thing contains the reason for its existence and the means by which the completeness of that existence shall be attained. Absolute cause is a quality common to the highest parts of compounds, for it contains the complete reason for the compound.

Government, according to causes, is government by the self; the whole administers the parts. Government, according to effect, is government by and of the parts, without participation in the conviction of wholeness. Growth is an extension of faculties toward the consciousness of cause, and ends in identification with cause as a spiritual experience. Any creature that accomplishes conscious identification with the principle of self attains the knowledge of the absolute cause of its own existence as a creature.

Superior and Inferior Natures

All superior natures stand in the relationship of causes to inferior natures. The sciences, for example, depend upon their superior, which is philosophy, for the perfection of themselves. Therefore philosophy stands as a cause in relationship to material learning. Deprived of philosophy, which includes morality and ethics, the sciences are left without a purpose superior to themselves. That which is without purpose beyond itself becomes the enemy of its own action. That which exists as a means to an end greater than itself advances toward union with superiors. This advance is essential progress.

Philosophy, in turn, may exist either as end or as means. Philosophy as end is a form of abstract intellectual gymnastics—the strengthening of faculties for their own sake—a procedure which results in the conflict of energized faculties active without reference to pattern. Philosophy as means is the organization of the rational powers toward the discovery of truth, which is the absolute of learning.

As the mind matures under philosophic discipline it becomes aware of its own dependence upon that which is beyond mind. This realization of dependence achieves a negative definition of that upon which the mind depends. By this negative definition the intellect becomes cognizant of consciousness as directly superior to itself. The true estate of philosophy is thus revealed. It is the means to the accomplishment of its own immediately superior state—the state of consciousness.

Platonic philosophy points out that the human being is connected with the universal order about him by a series of bridges called faculties. These faculties ascend in quality from the most physical to the most spiritual. Physical faculties serve as links between the internal man and the physical world; mental faculties as links between the internal man and the intellectual world, and spiritual faculties as links between the internal man and the world of causes. The physical and intellectual faculties are developed sufficiently to be understood, at least in part; but the majority of mankind is not yet aware of the existence of spiritual faculties. Even those who have attained the awareness that such faculties do exist, are unlearned and unskilled in their use. Neoplatonism taught that there is an exact science for the training of spiritual faculties by which they can be organized as instruments for the ultimate human purpose—the perception of causes.

Ancient India is the probable source of the exercises and disciplines used in the training of spiritual faculties. These exercises and disciplines are an important part of the so-called esoteric tradition. Academic thinkers may resent the implications of a secret over-science of the soul, but unless this over-science exists, all other learning is purposeless. Learning is vain unless it results in the state of being learned—that is, wise. Wisdom cannot exist apart from the knowledge of causes. Causes are unknowable in terms of our present intellectual equipment; therefore additional faculties must exist by which the end of learning is rendered possible.

Neoplatonism differed from Christianity in one philosophical particular. It insisted that the development of the spiritual faculties was possible only after the development of the material and intellectual faculties. Consciousness crowns learning, and is possible only to those who have perfected themselves to receive it.

Consciousness is present everywhere throughout nature, but manifests only according to the quality of the organisms which make up the body of nature. Therefore consciousness, though in itself perfect order, is perceived outwardly as a conflict of contending forms variously afflicting each other. Consciousness likewise is present everywhere in the constitution of man, but until the human being perfects his own organization this consciousness is perceived only in the conflict of functions, attitudes, opinions, and emotions. A state of spiritual security is not possible to man or nature until the patterns for that security have been set up by evolutionary processes, the highest of which is the self-discipline possible only to man.

There is no philosophical ground for the doctrine that consciousness can miraculously transmute a corrupt form by faith, belief, or affirmation. The inconsistencies between the idealistic codes of religious organizations and the behavior patterns of their members result from the false belief that the acceptance of a truth is identical in merit with the experiencing of that truth. The acceptance of that which has not been experienced is valuable only to the degree that it stimulates effort to experience. An abstract doctrine may inspire but it cannot perfect unless its laws are accepted as the basis of self-discipline.

From these and many other profound considerations the Neoplatonists formulated their pattern of the philosophic life. No other school of Western thought has approached the transcendent dignity of the Neoplatonic program of human regeneration.

Because they dared to extend their idealism into the secret world of causes, these Alexandrian transcendentalists have been accused of being addicted to magic, sorcery, and extravagant mysticism. The criticism is based on a single premise; namely, that man possesses no faculties beyond the intellect, and mysticism is a complicated form of self-delusion. Neoplatonism ceased as an independent school not because its teachings were disproved but because its doctrines were incomprehensible to those intellectuals who had no conception of wisdom as an experience of consciousness.

After nearly eighteen centuries of materialistic science and philosophy, the average man and woman is beginning to realize the deficiency of our traditional viewpoint on the subject of knowledge. The absurdity of the present situation is apparent especially to those whose minds have not been infected by the prevailing skepticism. The individual is asking himself what he needs in order to give purpose to his own life. Industry, economics, the trades, professions, arts, and crafts are means of survival, and are useful channels for the dissemination of culture. We are making a variety of adjustments to secure the necessities and luxuries of living. In time we may organize our social state into a comparatively smooth and well-running machine. When this is accomplished the utopian dream of socialized security may be fulfilled. We will live longer and better. But one question remains. According to our present program with all its advantages and promises, why live at all?

Life as we know it is at best a tempest in a teapot; much ado about nothing. We work that we may eat, and eat that we may work. Then someone recommends that we devise a plan to eat without working. The thought is intriguing, but not solutional. Life, no matter how we live it, will remain unendurable until we discover a purpose worthy of our mettle. We attain the brotherhood of man by binding men together in the voluntary service of superiors.

Even materialistic thinkers are beginning to suspect the existence of extrasensory perceptions. It is no longer scientific heresy to suggest that there may be more to man than shows upon the surface. A physicist said not long ago, "It is no longer possible to state empirically that man has no functions or faculties beyond those with which we are familiar." Cautious, but indicative, describes the viewpoint. If man does possess extrasensory faculties, does it not naturally follow that these faculties must be applied to the primary purposes of man—the extension of his power and dominion?

Neoplatonic philosophy not only postulated extrasensory faculties but declared that such faculties exist in all human beings. These latent faculties can be stimulated into activity, trained and directed, and used not only to increase our knowledge of externals but to intensify our realization of internals. The real end of philosophy is the stimulation and release of superior faculties. When philosophy lost this vision, when philosophers were content to argue the merits and demerits of conflicting schools, the whole body of philosophy lost the name of action. Thinking for the sake of thinking is not solutional of the world's dilemma. Intellectuals may enjoy a battle of wits, but this recreation is a luxury unsuited to the tempo of our times. We are in the presence of great decisions. We require a dynamic restatement of practical idealism. Individuals, communities, nations, races, and humanity as a whole, stand in desperate need of a vision beyond the limitations of the obvious. Our intellectual way of life has not rescued us or our institutions from the dismal pattern of war, crime, poverty, and disease. As things stand today we utterly lack the internal vision necessary to reform external conditions.

Neoplatonism is not a new and untried remedy for the prevailing distemper. As a formal pattern in the sphere of mind it has been unfolding for nearly seventeen hundred years. The current of its conviction has flowed from generation to generation, everywhere making fertile the seeds of human aspirations. The great leaders of world thought, philosophers, priests, statesmen, scientists, artists, and poets, have been Neoplatonists by conviction if not by formal acknowledgment. Idealists must forever rescue the world from the tragic consequences of materialism. The true leaders of our race have never labored merely for their own security or advancement. Their works have sprung from a secret conviction in themselves; they have been dedicated to the service of universals. To each of them a sovereign, invisible reality, stronger than any visible consideration, has sustained them through persecution, adversity, and martyrdom. They have derived their strength not from their world nor from the applause of the uninformed; their strength is from within. They were superior men and women because they approached by extension of consciousness the knowledge of causes. They discovered by experience the sovereignty of unity over diversity; the sovereignty of eternity over time. They built not for their own time but for the future; not for themselves but for all men; not for the world but beyond the world. Dare we say that these men were not practical?

This growth of truth and beauty in man, this mystical experience by which we share for an instant in the purpose for ourselves; this awakening from the dream of matter to the conscious state of spirit; this is Neoplatonism. If we would be happy, if we would justify our existence in terms of essential achievement, if we would rise from the uncertainty of opinion to the certainty of fact, let us make philosophy our journey.

This growth of truth and beauty in man, this mystical experience by which we share for an instant in the purpose for ourselves; this awakening from the dream of matter to the conscious state of spirit; this is Neoplatonism. If we would be happy, if we would justify our existence in terms of essential achievement, if we would rise from the uncertainty of opinion to the certainty of fact, let us make philosophy our journey.